HOW TO

Raise Children of DESTINY

HOW TO

Raise Children of DESTINY

DR. PATRICIA MORGAN

Unless otherwise indicated, all Scripture quotations are from the King James Version (KJV) of the Bible.

Scripture quotations marked (NIV) are from the Holy Bible, *New International Version,* © 1973, 1978, 1984 by the International Bible Society. Used by permission.

Scripture quotations marked (NKJV) are taken from the *New King James Version,* © 1979, 1980, 1982 by Thomas Nelson, Inc. Used by permission. All rights reserved.

HOW TO RAISE CHILDREN OF DESTINY

ISBN: 0-88368-561-2
Printed in the United States of America

Whitaker House
30 Hunt Valley Circle
New Kensington, PA 15068
web site: www.whitakerhouse.com

Library of Congress Cataloging-in-Publication Data

Morgan, Patricia, Dr.
How to raise children of destiny / Patricia Morgan.
p. cm.
Originally published: Shippensburg, PA : Destiny Image, ©1994.
ISBN 0-88368-561-2 (trade paper : alk. paper)
1. Parenting—Religious aspects—Christianity. I. Title.
BV4529.M644 2003
248.8'45—dc21

2002155426

1 2 3 4 5 6 7 8 9 10 11 12 / 12 11 10 09 08 07 06 05 04 03

Dedication

To Cathy, our firstborn, as you continue to display leadership to your brothers, and as you strategize for the children of the nation that you love so much, your Jamaica. The other nations also wait.

To Colin, our firstborn son, as you assume priestly leadership of the people of God. For this purpose you were born—to display the warm love and care of the Father as only you can do.

To Carrington, our second-born son, as you continue to discipline your body and mold your spirit to assume your authority as a wise man and counselor to the body of Christ.

To Christopher, our third-born son, as you continue to sharpen your skills and deepen your awareness of that strong call of God upon your life to minister as a prophet to your nation.

To Frantzler, our son-in-law, whose love for his people makes him eager to see all their oppression lifted. You are well able to set all your French-speaking people free!

To Chetsie-Challah my first grandchild, as you are carefully groomed to bring leadership to Haiti, and to lead your generation with regal grace, unmatched strength, and great wisdom.

And to Chetsie's children and grandchildren, who themselves will inherit generational blessings and generational responsibilities for God's kingdom on the earth.

And to my nations' children: I am determined to present you to God your Father as His delight and heritage.

Acknowledgments

My Father God, whose eyes I follow as they closely watch His children grow, for continuing to show me more of His father's heart.

His Son Jesus, who with obedience walked purposefully, determined to do what He was born to do—set mankind free.

The Holy Spirit, for His patience and encouragement as I collaborate with Him in the commission to raise my nation's children.

Dearest Peter, my husband-man and the father of my children, for his leadership, covering, and partnership with me in displaying the Father's glory to our generation and in raising up our children to do so in their generation.

Oral and Richard Roberts, whose transgenerational anointing I have admiringly observed and which displays the theme of this book.

My friends in ministry, Cynthia Townsend, Bishop and Mrs. Joseph Garlington, the pastors of all the Covenant Community Churches, and my colleagues from the International Third World Leaders Association led by Dr. Myles Munroe, whose fatherhood of their nations is my inspiration.

My mother, Louise, who led the way in her vigorous concern for her children, for her prayers for our family, directing the Father's blessings from generation to generation.

Contents

Foreword

"That our sons may be as plants grown up in their youth; that our daughters may be as pillars, sculptured in palace style."
—Ps. 144:12 NKJV

It is difficult to avoid the intensity of her feelings for the issue of raising children of destiny. Her passion for this subject and almost any other that one discusses with her is the most recognizable emotion I encounter in our conversations. Half measures are never sufficient, and I'm always struck by her sense of urgency as she contends for the wealth God has entrusted to us in our children.

Dr. Patricia Morgan is not a novice in this present discussion of a generation that yet needs to be challenged to fulfill their destiny. This ordained minister is a mother, a grandmother, and the wife to a significant apostolic trail-blazer renowned in the Caribbean and in international circles of ministry. She is both a brilliant educator and a riveting orator who has a burning passion to see *all* children brought to full purpose as God created them.

I have known and admired her for more than two decades. Her vision for "building daughters" and "planting sons" has grown immeasurably as her spheres of influence and opportunity have increased. I watched, one evening in our church, as we brought young people to the platform and she began to question them and their parents, utilizing her Individualized Purpose Plan. It was amazing to see what she could elicit from an eight-year-old boy who was being raised by a single mother.

Dr. Morgan's deep conviction for challenging every parent to raise children of destiny is birthed from the scriptural principle that emphasizes the uniqueness of every child created in the Father's image. *Uniqueness* is the operative word, and it should guide the process by which we pursue the Father's purpose for our children. One of my favorite lines in the movie, *Chariots of Fire*, is when Eric Liddell said, "When God made me, He made me fast; and when I run, I feel His pleasure." This must be the goal for every child, that when fully engaged in their created purpose, they too will feel the pleasure of God.

For years, I heard quoted—and often quoted myself—the passage in Proverbs 22:6, *"Train up a child in the way he* ***should*** go...." The emphasis was always on the *"should"* in the text; one day as I was meditating on this verse, I emphasized the word *"he."* I later discovered that the Amplified Bible had already made the discovery before me. Listen to it as you read it aloud:

> *Train up a child in the way he should go [and in keeping with his individual gift or bent], and when he is old he will not depart from it.*

In a world where "politically correct" language and images are constantly bombarding us from every conceivable angle, we are mandated to hear afresh this prophetic message to the redeemed community. We cannot let the world press us into its mold, but we must set our course for a horizon that is sparkling with the variegated hues and colors of that generation spoken of by the psalmist:

> *Let this be written for a future generation, that a people not yet created may praise the* LORD. (Ps. 102:18 NIV)

I encourage you to drink deeply of these words and then seek to employ them with prayer, vision, faith, and vigor.

Bishop Joseph L. Garlington, Ph.D.
Senior Pastor
Covenant Church of Pittsburgh
President
Reconciliation! Ministries International

Introduction

"What we need more than anything else is not textbooks but text-people. It is the personality of the teacher which is the text that the pupils read, the text they will never forget." [1]

The next generation will not be fathered by persuasive pulpiteers and public orators, but by committed adults who will spend quality time with their children, imparting life both by instruction and by example.

While more than 60 percent of the world's population is under twenty-five years of age, the number of casualties among them is alarming. Drugs, sex, and crime have twisted their minds and drained their bodies. They have been left incarcerated or abandoned to roam crowded city streets and expend their energies in wanton waste.

The facade of yesterday's "wood, hay, and stubble" (see 1 Corinthians 3:12) has left today's youth stumbling along with their own uncertain values, permissiveness, purposelessness, and promiscuity. Now this *orphaned generation* is reducing its cultural heritage to ashes.

---

[1] Abraham J. Herchel, "The Spirit of Jewish Education," Jewish Education 24/2 Fall, 1953/:19.

The most urgent prophetic voice, which is fitting for today, was that of Elijah, who longed to *"turn the hearts of the fathers to their children, and the hearts of the children to their fathers; or else I will come and strike the land with a curse"* (Mal. 4:6 NIV).

This book sounds that same prophetic cry. It is a call to fathers and mothers, pastors and teachers, and church and civic leaders to spend quality time with our children. It is a follow-up to the author's previous book, *The Battle for the Seed* and an information manual accompanying her book *The Cry of the Children.* It is a practical guide on how to train our children in the principles and values of the Word of God. Each child, as a unique creature, must discover his purpose, release his potential, and sharpen his skills to become a productive and fulfilled citizen to the glory of God.

At a time when the secular state has taken center stage in the education process, *How to Raise Children of Destiny* takes us back to the generational responsibility of home and church. It is restoring the pride and confidence in our historical, spiritual, and ethical Judeo-Christian heritage.

The Jewish Mishnah advises the youth, "Let your house be a meeting-place for the sages, and sit in the very dust at their feet, and thirstily drink in their words" (Abot 1:4). Jesus Christ, in Matthew 28:19–20 (NIV) made clear our responsibility to *"make disciples of all nations."* The method is *"teaching them."* The purpose is to *"obey everything* [the Lord has] *commanded."*

Dr. Pat Morgan writes within this biblical tradition, bringing to this work the authority of experience, detailed research, and prophetic insight. She has raised four children of her own. She has made a determined decision that her daughter (Cathy) and three sons (Colin, Carrington, and Christopher) should exceed their parents. Inspired by the notion that it takes three generations to change a nation, she has committed herself to be a part of the first. Her grandchildren will see the fulfillment of her vision and her ministry.

Dr. Pat Morgan's professional discipline as a university instructor and respected consultant in special education and Christian school education adds credibility to her work.

In this book, you meet a mother with a prophetic heart, rising up from the rich culture of the "third world" to challenge every man's world and to collaborate with God in the battle for the seed.

I am proud to be her husband.

—Rev. Dr. Peter Morgan

1
The Abortion of Vision

I felt as if I was watching a brutal execution. With bowed heads, hundreds of teenagers waited before an altar like humble sheep, ready to lay down their lives.

Suddenly, with an upraised voice that cut through the air like a giant executioner's sword, the preacher on the stage put on his best eschatological pose and proclaimed with a flourish of somber finality, "You are the *last generation!*"

As those cruel words of doom fell on the young people, I could sense their silent shock of surprise. The pain of those damning words struck their yielded hearts and pierced their souls to the core. Only God knows how many youthful dreams, visions, and aspirations died in that place that day.

I'll never forget that scene. It moved me, more than any other, to write this book. The young people at the altar that day were eager and optimistic about devoting the rest of their lives to serving Jesus. Only moments before, they had raced toward the altar and bared their hearts in shameless vulnerability before a seemingly trustworthy adult shepherd. Those teenagers needed goals and direction, and they needed avenues for service.

The preacher had planned it all; the rousing sermon led to a dynamic call to recommit themselves to God. The altar call was made; the net was thrown out and the fish were pulled in. The heart-hungry teens came to the altar in droves. Which of these young people would not want to come forward in dedication to God when this fine man so eloquently articulated His call?

With bowed heads, hundreds of young hearts waited to seal their devotion with the minister's prayer of consecration. Then, at the peak of their potential and zeal, they were robbed of their dreams with one tired and pompous religious phrase: *"You are the last generation!"*

As parents and educators, *we must not withhold from our children the greatest gift and inheritance we possess—the gift of hope! Jesus Christ did not command us to hold the future of our children hostage until He returns.* God forbid! He commanded, *"Go ye therefore, and teach all nations"* (Matt. 28:19), and *"Go ye into all the world, and preach the gospel to every creature"* (Mark 16:15).

Our living Hope has made a permanent deposit in our hearts that activates and energizes God-directed faith and action. By living in fear and "suspended anticipation," we presumptuously bankrupt the hope of our children and their children after them!

The purposes of God are eternal. Empowered by God's will and Word, those purposes will be accomplished on the earth—but not by fearful Christians huddled in lush strongholds awaiting rescue from a terrible world that seems to threaten the very strength and power of their God! No! God's divine intention for His creation is *sovereign rulership.* That rulership demands generations of God's righteous seed who will inherit the God-given right to dominion and authority.

Instead of cutting off the inheritance of the Lord through our ignorance and fear, we must *actively strategize* for the future of our children, as the wise woman in 2 Samuel 20 did. If we save our seed, we will also preserve our cities and nations by our wise assessment of the enemy's devices and through our radical and personal commitment to action and deliverance.

God's perspective should be our perspective. God *has already* risen in the earth. Jesus Christ is *already* victorious over His enemies. He is still building *"his sanctuary* [the church] *like high palaces, like the earth which he hath established for ever"* (Ps. 78:69).

The adults of the body of Christ must be *prepared* for this twenty-first century. Careless indifference, hopeless despair, and the shortcut maneuvers we've adopted, which are based on an eschatology of disaster and escapism, cannot be tolerated any longer. Neither will God accept our caustic scorn for the world and its sin and failure, or our "better-than-thou" haughty spirituality and prophetic posturing.

While the church builds higher walls to hide its growing fears, the great minds of the world are hard at work seeking answers. Yes, they seek solutions outside of God in their ignorance, but at least they are rising to the call of the masses for assessment, prognosis, and answers. They refuse to yield to hopelessness. They are determined to find solutions to their global questions.

As godless historians, sociologists, environmentalists, and politicians alike diligently offer their answers, they display a *far greater sense of responsibility* than do the God-appointed leaders of the body of Christ! What a shame! Jesus Christ made it clear that we bear direct responsibility for being salt and light to the world of men and nations (Matt. 5:13–16).

Paul Kennedy, author of *Preparing for the Twenty-First Century* (1993), attempted to produce answers to national and international problems. Determined to provide answers for the survival of the human race, he offered many solutions, including "inventive capitalism," "increased development aid," "mass production from solar energy for use in developing countries," "cheap contraceptive devices for women," and "re-education" to help people "think more globally."[1]

In an interview, Kennedy alluded to the difficulty he faced as he sought answers for the problems we now face. He actually stated that one possible conclusion, after considering his mass of data about global conditions, was one of *despair.* Then he commented that a position of despair would not help his fifteen-year-old son. This social theoretician was concerned about the future of his seed. He refused to bow to despair. His compulsion then was toward *hope,* not *despair.*

Many avid researchers of God's Word, acclaimed leaders of the body of Christ, and parents of the next generation respond to the world's problems with a "doom and gloom" mentality and a posture of failure and despair. Unbelieving and godless researchers appear to exhibit a greater sense of responsibility and concern for the next generation than we do. They respond with hope and determination to preserve their seed. Who is going to be right in their prognosis and approach toward the twenty-first century? Will it be "the people of hope" who exhibit no hope, or "the people without hope" who *do* exhibit hope—even apart from Christ? And what of their stated reason to hope? "Our children must survive!"

Christian Parents Must Discern the Times

The sons of Issachar were honored and given special mention in God's Word for their discernment. *"And of the children of Issachar, which were men that had understanding of the times, to know what Israel ought to do"* (1 Chron. 12:32). We are the caretakers of God's seed, His inheritance in the earth. He gave us children for His own purposes, not merely for our personal enjoyment and fulfillment. For their sakes and

[1] Paul Kennedy, *Preparing for the Twenty-First Century* (New York: Random House, 1993).

ours, it is time for us to accurately perceive the mind of God through His Spirit. This involves at least five steps:

1. In-depth research into the *original, eternal, and universal plan* of God concerning His *overall master plan for His world of men and nations.*
2. Continued development of our knowledge of the *mind* of the God of covenant and promise, and of His *purpose* and *divine intention* for eternity to guide our daily lives.
3. A deeper understanding of God as a *generational God* whose divine *modus operandi* (method of operation) is to invest His eternal hope in the next generation, the seed that is yet within the loins of the adult church. Our Father God has chosen to place His *hope* for succeeding generations in the seed of His church, just as He placed every hope for our future in the seed of David, Jesus Christ, and in those believers who would follow after Him.
4. Our determined decision to *collaborate with God* in the *salvation of the world* based upon His mandated ministry of reconciliation. This decision presupposes an *assumption of responsibility* on man's part and a *delegation of authority* on God's part. This authority, and our ability to wield it, is fueled by our *recreative nature* on the one hand (our God-given ability to reproduce after our own kind), and on the other, by our strong and determined will to both *survive* and *preserve our seed.* (See Genesis 1:26–28.)
5. Accurate assessment of problems. Our assessment must not be based on a circular, insular, or introverted examination of global conditions. Our judgment must be based on a broader perspective. It should be more longitudinal, linear, eternal, and optimistic because our perspective is based on God's original plan and His determination to see His purposes fulfilled. God only has one posture

toward our world: He is simply and totally God—the God of the universe. And His posture is eternal, positive, and necessarily optimistic!

If we fulfill these prerequisites, we will find ourselves propelled beyond our narrow cause-and-effect vision (which is restricting and short-term), pushed into God's future, and required to operate the way God does.

God demands a radical change from a man-centered frame of reference to one that is God-centered. Man-centered thinking says, in effect, "Man sins...man is punished...Jesus dies for man...man tries in vain...man fails...Jesus again has to make a dramatic rescue move on man's behalf [because He failed the first time]."

The God-centered frame of reference declares, "God purposes...God creates in perfection...God provides for restoration...God fulfills His promise through His Son...God's Son completely fulfills God's plan for the establishment of His kingdom among men and nations...God's people willingly collaborate with Him in the salvation of God's world and take up active positions of joint rulership and responsibility. Furthermore, they prepare the next generation for continued collaboration with God."

Is it possible for us to become the generation of the body of Christ that learns to see beyond the failures of the human race? Will we see beyond our selfish and self-imposed verdict of "perpetual guilt and imperfection by nature and by default" to the abundant life we have received in Christ? (See John 10:10.)

Will we dare to move beyond our pseudo-spiritual, global confession of failure, and wholesale surrender of the culture to the world? Will we move beyond our laying down of the corporate will of the body of Christ to a God-ordained position in a place of victory based squarely on our knowledge of God's determination?

When we stubbornly refuse to budge from our ringside seat at the "apocalypse arena," we doom our children through our disobedience and force them to resign themselves to life as "the last generation." Are we prepared to tell them how to pray when they have no future to pray about? Why should they eagerly run to pursue such a hollow prize? How can we expect our children to focus their God-given zeal on the "privilege" of dragging their feet in time to the sluggish beat of the rapture-waiting adults around them?

While God wants our seed to dream of great exploits accomplished for and through Him, we seem to be actually pressing them to give up all thoughts of marriage, ministry, and vision—"After all, there won't be time!"

We lower the ceiling on our children's lives every time we pompously assume we understand God's will so well that we can name the time of His coming and tell our children, "You are the last generation!" How can they contain their life's dreams in the few short remaining years we give them?

As an educator, a parent, and a minister of the gospel, I am expected by God to be an optimist. I am to expect the highest and best from my students, my children, and my flock. You and I alike are required by our eternal God to have a long-term view. Regardless of our end-time views or theology, we should live holy lives as if Christ will knock at our doors tonight, yet dream for the next generation and build to last for centuries.

True optimism is built solely on a knowledge of God's purposes and acts. I am confident that my students will accomplish the goals God has predetermined for them if they have the blessing and promise of *time* within their grasp and the future before them, accompanied by the optimistic guidance of significant adults.

I find it difficult to understand the attitudes of many so-called spokespersons of the church today. I am offended when I see these leaders assume responsibility for teaching our young, and yet dare to approach the task with "ceilings" and preconceived limitations. They oppress, limit, and quench the dreams of their young charges with the weight of their own hopelessness, and enslave them with their self-made limitations.

I must bluntly say that if a "minister" of the Gospel cannot offer optimism to those of the next generation, then he should be kept away from them. If he has no answer for the decay in our nations, if he feels helpless and has no anointed word for the next generation, then he should be forbidden to speak his own hopelessness to our children.

The truth is that God has ordained the church to preserve the world through its saltiness. The modern church has lost its saltiness and its "leavening" powers. It has allowed itself to be overcome by the perceived magnitude of the unleavened, unredeemed dough. It has forgotten the power of just a little leaven to leaven the whole loaf. (See Matthew 13:33.)

Many Christian leaders believe that the growth of the tares has outstripped that of the wheat, and some have even taken it upon themselves to announce the advent of the reaper who will put the sickle to both wheat and tares!

These leaders seem to have relegated the responsibility of the church (which is to be life, salt, light, and leaven to this generation) to some ultimate transcendental move of Jesus Christ who, with one fell swoop, will descend, defeat our enemy (again), and reign, thus getting us off the hook.

What of the life of Christ within us? Does His life completely enwrap and inflame us? What did the apostle Paul mean when he told the members of the church at Philippi, *"That ye may be blameless and harmless, the sons of God, without rebuke, in the midst of a crooked and perverse nation, among whom ye shine as lights in the world"* (Phil. 2:15)? The life of Christ within us fully equips us for victory *"according as his divine power hath given unto us all things that pertain unto life and godliness, through the knowledge of him that hath called us to glory and virtue*" (2 Pet. 1:3).

When the articulate leaders of Christ's body cry, "I surrender!" to the enemy, what do they expect Jesus Christ to do? Will our escapist mentality, our caustic disgust of the world God so loves, or our preparation for His imminent return manage to "force" Him to return? Will our playful juggling of dates, times, and seasons produce a situation in which the Father will have to redeem us again by sending His Son for the second time lest the church be made a laughingstock?

The leaders and prognosticators of Christ's imminent return must ask themselves, "Do I have a short-term goal (six years or so) just so I can frantically call my people to repentance? Am I choosing to believe this way because it's easier for me to preach a traditional message of 'salvation' rather than to methodically educate my adults, their children, and their children's children into the life of Christ?"

This generation in the body of Christ has become very self-centered, with an inordinate compulsion to "succeed." We have stocked our bookshelves and equipped each other with easy recipes for success in the kingdom. A little faith here and a little Word there! Yet we have had little drive to rouse ourselves and plan for the future. Why? It's too painful to plan for the future!

If only we can waylay those creditors for just a little longer. We have that large debt on our new 5,000-seat auditorium, so don't require us to plan an inheritance for our children, and certainly not for our children's children—after all, Jesus is coming soon!

We need to examine our fears and our deepest motivations. We must remind ourselves that we serve a God of hope and promise, a God of generations. By His very nature He is victorious, optimistic, futuristic, and long-term.

God's nature is eternal. His Word and covenant promises are eternal. He is raising up men and women who are prepared to optimistically battle for the salvation of a wicked city or the survival of a nation.

God is not a loser! He is the ultimate winner who has made every provision for our complete victory. God's Word foretold that Jesus Christ would set up and reign over a kingdom that will be eternal (Dan. 2:35, 44; Isa. 2:2; Ps. 80:9).

He has made us kings and priests (Rev. 1:6), and He is calling forth a righteous nation of kings that will execute justice and judgment on the earth (Prov. 21:3; Jude 15). He has given us promises that require our present-day acceptance and assertion of our responsibility on the earth.

A Hope and Plan for Our Children

God has planted eternity in our hearts. That eternity is bound up in our children and in our children's children. God has ordained that our seed—our children—inherit the earth (Ps. 25:13; 69:35–36). Our children were conceived to reign and judge the earth. They will stand on the prophetic words they have received and execute God's purposes on the earth.

Amos 2:10–12 gives us a striking picture that illustrates the importance (and eternal effects) of our actions. God has given us divine promises for our children. He said that He would raise them up as prophets to their generation. Woe unto us if He comes to us with the accusation, "But you commanded the prophets saying, 'Prophesy not!'" (See Amos 2:12.)

God commands us to bless our children (Num. 6:23–27), but we withhold our blessing. Why? A prophetic word for our children propels us into the future, and we are afraid of the future! When we withhold our blessings from the next generation, we are depriving our children of the direction and resources that will determine the history of our own nation.

We stifle the life of righteous seed within our wombs. We stifle the life of the seed of a prophetic word in our spirits because a prophetic word may well make demands on us today, and well into this twenty-first century! We dare to declare to the next generation, *"You are the last generation!"*

God created us in His image; He has ordained that we share His nature. God has to be optimistic and long-term. He has to do what His eternal nature demands. He has fathered sons and daughters, and His father's heart longs to see His seed grow up and present more sons and daughters to Him, His heritage! He cannot afford to conform to our fearful, cowardly expectations. His own divine hope for the salvation of the world and for the establishment of His kingdom is wrapped up in the survival of our children (Isa. 44:3; Ps. 112:1–2).

God's kingdom is an everlasting kingdom that extends from generation to generation (Dan. 4:3). Our failure to perceive God's nature and purpose for our children is postponing the establishment of God's kingdom.

I visited a Christian high school attended by some of the finest, cream-of-the-crop young Christian students in America. I noticed a strange phenomenon taking place in those bright young people, both consciously and unconsciously. Once these young students heard some "significant" adult voices begin to jump on the bandwagon and boldly articulate and announce dates for Christ's return, the students quickly developed a *qué será será* ("what will be, will be") apathy toward spiritual things and an intoxicating hunger for heightened carnal experiences and "quick-fix" solutions to daily problems.

Teachers began to overhear statements such as, "Well, I don't have to get married. Why get married? The Bible says, 'Woe unto them that are with child in those days,' (see Matthew 24:19) so I don't want any children. Well, why plan to go to a university? My father says he doesn't see how he can afford it anyway. Let's eat, drink, and be merry, because tomorrow it's all over. We can't win anyway; so why try?"

This ugly phenomenon is taking hold of our young people. This subtle and fatal disease is robbing them of their optimism and their willingness to prepare for their leadership positions in the body of Christ and in their nations.

When adult leaders declare failure and Christian leaders have no answers, our children not only direct their pain and disillusionment toward us as their parents, but they are also forced to "foreclose" on their own future! We are unleashing a lethal weapon over the heads of the next generation, a weapon of mass genocide—not of a generation, but of a generation's hopes for the future. We are killing their God-given visions and dreams. We will be held responsible for our part in this tragedy.

I call upon parents and educators, seed-bearers and seed preservers, and teachers of the next generation to jealously guard the spirits of our children. Our future is wrapped up in theirs. Let us pass on the kingdom to the next generation and let us do it lavishly, fully, and unselfishly. Let us prophesy over and bless our children with dreams that demand hopeful expectation and time!

This is not the end of time, but an hour of transition. Older leaders must train and begin to give way to the new generation of leaders. Pastors must begin to pass on God's prophetic intention for His people to the next generation. As parents and teachers, we must invest generously in our children by providing direction for their dreams. We must lavishly bestow the greatest of all gifts: hope in the God of our fathers and in Jesus Christ, who shall see His seed, who shall prolong His days, and in whose hand the pleasure of the Lord shall prosper (Isa. 53:10).

2
Your Seed: The Hope of Your Nation

I see it in the eyes of my people's children—the will to live and the determination to succeed,
A quiet but strong boldness to defend themselves from the enemy without, and still to win.

National deliverance begins with the birth of a child! Whenever a nation is in trouble, God causes a deliverer to be born! The births of a nation's delivering children mark the birth of hope in the history of that nation. God's *modus operandi* is to place within any organism He has created a means of defending itself against external attacks. If a nation is a family of families, and if children bear the life-regenerating responsibility of families for the next generation, then God has endowed our children with the ability to deliver their nations!

Moses is a perfect example of God's nation-saving work among men. The life of Moses clearly reveals the hand of God at work as He designed the purpose of three children (Moses, Aaron, and Miriam), and the collaborative responsibility of their parents.

God heard the anguished cry of the Hebrews enslaved by the Egyptians, and He intervened with the inconspicuous birth of a Hebrew boy. At the same time, Pharaoh acted to curb the growth of the Hebrew people by issuing an order, first to the midwives and then to all the people, to destroy every male Hebrew newborn by drowning. (See Exodus 1:15–22). He did not realize that God Himself had ordained a historic counterattack that would years later end in the Pharaoh's death and the death of his firstborn son.

God's strategy to preserve His people and establish His kingdom on earth has always involved children. Before the foundation of the world, God had a plan. The second chapter of Exodus begins with what appears to be just a casual, introductory phrase. However, it reveals the intricate and designing activity of the Lord God in the affairs of men. *"And there went a man of the house of Levi, and took to wife a daughter of Levi. And the woman conceived, and bare a son"* (Exod. 2:1–2).

Does this passage seem commonplace? Notice how God brought together the seed of two members of the priestly tribe of Levi (the inheritor of all of the strengths, training, and heritage of his forefathers) to form a deliverer! Moses, and God's plan for Israel's deliverance, was born.

God planted in Moses a predisposition to become Israel's national liberator. How was this done?

1. God conditioned Moses' heart and perception through the events surrounding his birth, including the ruthless slaughter of the male babies of his generation. The mother of Moses nursed him and certainly rehearsed the story of his own miraculous escape from death again and again. In the end, this son raised in the house of Pharaoh nevertheless understood the anguish of his people, Israel.
2. Moses' priestly heritage preconditioned, shaped, and strengthened his desire to act on behalf of his people.

3. Moses' very name, which means "drawn from water," constantly reminded him of the holocaust of his generation. He was a survivor, but he carried within him the pain of the people.
4. Moses' upbringing in Pharaoh's household did not condition him to follow in Pharaoh's footsteps, for he could never truly become the son of Pharaoh (or the "son of a god"). Deeper, stronger, and more natural were his ties to his own people. His heart was set to defend those of his own race and to deliver them from bondage. *"And it came to pass in those days, when Moses was grown, that he went out unto his brethren, and looked on their burdens"* (Exod. 2:11).
5. God's dealings with Moses during the forty years he spent in the wilderness prepared him for the day God appeared to him, saying, *"I am the God of thy fathers"* (Exod. 3:6). Every day of Moses' training, God had listened to the people cry out in their bondage to Egypt. God remembered His covenant with their forefathers and moved on their behalf. He called forth the son He had prepared!

God always places children at the heart of a nation who are born to rise up and defend their nation. There is a parallel principle, as well, which is revealed in Exodus 4:22–23:

> *And thou shalt say unto Pharaoh, Thus saith the LORD, Israel is my son, even my firstborn: and I say unto thee, Let my son go, that he may serve me: and if thou refuse to let him go, behold, I will slay thy son, even thy firstborn.*

Consider the scene described in Exodus 4:22–23. Ask yourself the following questions:

1. Who are the protagonists?
2. Who are they fighting over?
3. Are children being slain today?

4. Does the Challenger still say the same to others who hold His prize in bondage today?

Your responses to these questions offer a measure of your knowledge of how God works and the extent to which you believe He will work on behalf of your children. Your answers will also, to some degree, explain the death of today's "firstborn sons of Egypt." Are you ready to stand by and watch the holocaust of the nation's children?

I am thankful that when I look into my children's eyes, I see a confidence and assurance there. By the grace of God, my husband and I have armed ourselves and confronted the enemy at every turn, so that our children will also have a chance to be *"more than conquerors"* (Rom. 8:37).

I am saddened, however, when I see in the words and actions of other children the growing evidence of a muffled sense of vision, a dulled sense of mission, and a blunted sense of call.

When I look for the leaders these children admire, I find only a few halfhearted heroes. Their messages are conflicting; their pedestals are precariously perched; and, worst of all, they are not willing to be examples. Even if they were, their uncertain messages would continue to be blatantly rejected because they lack strength, conviction, and proper execution.

I fear that this generation of children in nearly every nation is losing the battle for a meaningful future, partly because of the sheer weight of their parents' irresponsible dismissal of their nations' pain, and partly because of their heroes' failures to lead and model true vision. I fear that the few battles won by parents and teachers will not be recognized or remembered by the children.

We must teach our children to exalt God. His promises are for them to inherit. They must claim these promises as their own.

One of my greatest fears is that children will not exalt the God of their fathers. If we don't accept our responsibility to the next generation, I fear that, in the years to come, there will be no altars erected by optimistic godly fathers, no battle scars shown, and no one left to answer the eternal and probing question of the children, *"What meaneth this?"* (Acts 2:12).

Without fathers and mothers who know their God, proclaim His deliverance, and teach their children to follow Him, the children of tomorrow will not know the strength and power of the God of their fathers. They will not know the covenant promises confirmed by God's oath to their forefathers. They will not declare to their God, "As You spoke to our fathers, to Abraham, and to his seed forever, so bless me with my father's blessing." (See Luke 1:55.)

Will the neglected seed of this generation turn back as the children of Ephraim did in the day of battle—because they have forgotten the greatness of the God of their fathers? (See Psalm 78:9–11.) Even the secular press is calling this group of children "the lost generation"!

So much history! So great a heritage! Will it be lost and squandered through our selfishness and apathy? I am a Caribbean woman of Trinidad, married to a man of Jamaican parentage. As I think of the value of my Christian heritage, I can feel the drumbeats deep within my African spirit, and I can almost sense the great civilizations of my fathers' pasts. I want to say to my children, "This is your rich heritage. Drink deeply of it. For the blood of the free sank deeply into the ground of your fathers' God and still cries out to Him for the atonement of the priests of your generation—and you, my children, are those priests."

We must tell our children, our God-given seed of promise, "These promises and gifts are yours to inherit, so claim them as your own—the lavish worship of the priestly Melchisedec; the generous fatherhood of the patriarch Abraham; the warrior praises of the kingly David; Rahab's fearless will for her family's survival; Deborah's unyielding sense of justice in the face of impossible odds; the clarity of vision in the sons of Issachar; and the legendary swiftness of Cush."

All this you have within your blood, my children, and it all brings you the glorious heritage of the God of your fathers.

The enemy seeks to destroy your life, my strong and vibrant little ones. He seeks to muffle your cries, to take away the very voice you give to your pain. I hear it in your little songs.

And when I ask you, "What will you be when you grow up?" you hang your head in silence. Or you say you want to be a ballplayer!

Has no one reminded you of your heritage and that there is more? Has no one told you of the mission of your race? Has no one earmarked you for the greatness for which you were born?

I fear that we are losing the battle for the seed.

The Battle for the Seed

The great battle for the seed started long ago. Even before the foundations of the earth, God had already prepared a master plan for the salvation of the seed:

1. God Himself would be a Father.
2. He would give His only begotten Son, His "first fruit," as the Seed of our salvation.
3. God would make men generational in spirit, soul, and body.
4. Men were created, enabled, and commanded to produce offspring who would extend the work of God and of His Son upon the earth.
5. When Satan intruded and tempted man in his attempt to spoil the seed of God, the first man fell, apparently dooming the race to eternal separation from God. But

God, who created man ("Adam" in the original languages) in His image and planted him in the earth, set His divine plan into motion—initiating the battle for the seed!

6. The Bible account reveals a divine determination in the heart of our Father God for *"the seed of the woman"* to crush the head of Satan (Gen. 3:15). God the Creator ignited a divine imperative in the hearts of Adam and Eve to preserve their seed, to arm them for the battle, and to instill in them a sense of their purpose and a confidence about their certain victory.
7. God ordained that the success of His plan hinge upon one dominant factor: Man would have to arm himself with the mind of a Father God whose heritage is the children, whose divine hope is invested in righteous seed. This is the same God who dares Satan daily just as He dared Pharaoh: *"Israel is my son, even my firstborn: and I say unto thee, Let my son go, that he may serve me: and if thou refuse to let him go, behold, I will slay thy son, even thy firstborn"* (Exod. 4:22–23).

Don't be deceived. This battle for the seed is not just a symbolic spiritual idea. We are literally battling for our children! The battle is a head-on, bloody, literal, and on-going struggle between godly parents and an anti-Christ adversary for the future of the next generation.

In the Garden: The Declaration of War

We are the creations of a God of purpose. Everything He does has meaning and purpose. We need to understand that God created us with the ability to reproduce after our own kind. Beginning with Adam, the first of our kind, God made it clear that He created us—and the seed that follows us—to lead. The God of the universe is clearly determined to extend Himself and all that He is through His highest creation: man.

Our universe reflects elements of God's sovereign spirit in its divine order, structure, harmony, and balance. In the beginning, God exercised His divine rulership and moved by His Spirit upon His creation. This was simply the outward manifestation of movement in the creative "womb" of the family of the Father, the Son, and the Holy Spirit, a generative and procreative spirit.

A holy seed was born out of this divine covenant-love relationship and unity. From this spiritual seed was created a being who bore the Creator's image and likeness, a creature who would also provide for the generations of sons and daughters who would fellowship with the Holy Spirit.

After God said, *"Let us make man"* (Gen. 1:26), the great battle began as the jealousy and fears of the adversary were ignited. Adam, and his wife, Eve, were responsible for caring for the garden. They were given the commission and ability to maintain God's authority and dominion in the garden, and though they were human, they enjoyed daily communion with the Lord God.

According to the book of Genesis, God saw that His highest creation was good and that His eternal creature would accomplish the purpose for which he was created. The Creator God, knowing all things, also gave His creation specific instructions and warnings. He expected Adam and Eve to walk in obedience, subjecting even the rebellious Lucifer, whose inflated pride and jealousy craved for God's property, for God's authority and dominion in the garden.

God's prized creation became Satan's most coveted and vulnerable target. The seed of woman represented everything he had lost in his rebellion and everything he feared in his future. If he could corrupt this seed, if he could mar God's image and distort God's likeness in the earth, then he could gain man's submission and subvert man's dominion authority over the earth.

With cynical, divisive cunning, Satan took the form of a serpent and hissed, *"Hath God said?"* (Gen. 3:1). With alluring appeal to man's lust and pride, Satan tempted man. The battle for the seed of God had begun with this first attempt to gain man's allegiance.

Genesis 3:1–19 relates the apparent triumph of Satan and the effects of this battle on human history. Position yourself, if you can, in the mind of the Creator, the Father God. Now He must enact the generational plan He had prepared before the creation of our world. Out of Himself, He must provide the Seed of deliverance, His own Son, the Word who was with Him before the beginning. He had already determined that He would sacrifice His only begotten Son for the salvation of multiplied generations of sons and daughters.

At the same time, the fallen angel and former servant of God called Lucifer also desired seed, but he was doomed to reproduce rebellious seed after his own kind, who swore allegiance to him. The God of order would only operate according to His own nature and principles. He would strike a death blow to Satan's plan of separation and usurpation of God's fatherhood by causing His divine Seed to become flesh and enter the world as a man, as the promised Seed of the woman. God the Creator ordained what Satan desperately feared: This holy Seed would, in generations to come, bruise the head of Satan.

When God proclaimed, "The Seed of the woman will bruise your head" (see Genesis 3:15), Satan recoiled in the dust, and Adam and Eve emerged tall and strong. There was hope!

"And I will put enmity between thee and the woman" (Gen. 3:15). Surely God meant that He would rivet into man's spirit a natural, irreconcilable hostility against the seducer. When the Creator said, *"it* [woman's seed] *shall bruise thy head"* (Gen. 3:15), surely He referred to the total, irrevocable victory Jesus

won at Calvary, as well as the spoils our seed would claim in this life!

"The seed of the woman." Now we understand why God so indelibly stamped His image upon the seed of Adam and Eve. That image was to be recreated and reproduced, and therein lay the promise of victory.

It was through the power of their love and covenant relationship—their ability to cohabit and to deeply unite in love—that their unity would reproduce what God had created—a man-child stamped with the image of God. Within every child born on the earth would dwell a spirit imprinted with a natural affiliation with God the Father and a natural repulsion and hatred of the evil one. It would be through this seed of promise that God would restore man to full dominion authority, full sonship with Himself, and total mastery over Satan.

The Transformation of Man's Time Perspective

The words "the seed of the woman" reveal an eternal hope and promise invested in the seed, a certain knowledge of a miracle that was destined to come to pass in a generation to come.

A generation to come? Then that means the hope of man must be linked to God's hope—in generations! With this powerful proclamation, God drastically altered the time perspective of finite man.

In the beginning, Adam and Eve enjoyed a *timeless* Edenic fellowship with their eternal, infinite God. Evidently this relationship was meant to continue unbroken for all of eternity. Then the unchanging judgment of death cut short Eden's joy as Adam and Eve willfully crossed the only line God had given them: *"But of the tree of the knowledge of good and evil, thou shalt not eat of it: for in the day that thou eatest thereof thou shalt surely die"* (Gen. 2:17). Even before man's transgression, the all-knowing Creator had a plan. It included a glorious promise of seed passed from generation to generation over time—He would call into being those things which "were not" for a glorious purpose.

> *But God hath chosen the foolish things of the world to confound the wise; and God hath chosen the weak things of the world to confound the things which are mighty; and base things of the world, and things which are despised, hath God chosen, yea, and things which are not, to bring to nought things that are.* (1 Cor. 1:27–28)

Adam and Eve began to reckon time from the moment their eternal spirits felt the limits of life in physical bodies that were now doomed to die. But with the Father God's promise, their future seemed to stretch them beyond death into a new dimension through the infinite possibilities of their children, and their children's children after them. They must have experienced a new taste of the eternity that they had once experienced—but now they had to remember their past.

Surely they had to have a sense of the future and of their divine destiny. God's word had already been dispatched into that future. His powerful hope and purpose were energizing all things so His word would be fulfilled. All that remained was for the first man and his wife to perceive and receive their Creator's revelation. The very destiny of the human race was at stake: Would the first parents catch their Creator's vision for their seed? Would they take hold of their only hope and collaborate with their God in the outworking of their salvation?

We are here. We participate in God's kingdom because Adam and Eve did collaborate with God. So did countless individuals in the generations that followed them. Thus God, in partnership with His created firstborn, hastened to perform His Word. Now generations of seed have been raised up, and the promise of the Deliverer was fulfilled through the miraculous linking thread of generation after generation. Since our Deliverer's arrival and departure from our world, God continues to expand His kingdom in the earth through the same ancient plan that brought His Son: from generation to generation.

When Mary responded to the angel's astounding proclamation with the words, *"Behold the handmaid of the Lord; be it unto me according to thy word"* (Luke 1:38), the promise of God uttered in the garden of Eden became incarnate within her and the Deliverer of creation was conceived. The battle raged on as it had from generation to generation. Herod schemed and slaughtered many of man's seed, as many other tools of the adversary before him had also done. Satan blindly tempted and tried this Seed, but Jesus the Messiah was born to die. He was determined to *"declare his generation"* and to *"see his seed"* (Isa. 53:8, 10). He was destined before the foundation of the world to overcome him who had the power of death, to reclaim the keys of death and hell, and to take captivity captive!

The Battle Still Rages!

Satan still craves seed who bear God's image, who carry dominion ability, and who bear in their eternal spirits the God-implanted predisposition to crush his head! Satan's only hope to possess the power of domination he craves is to steal, kill, or destroy our seed! The seed of woman is the very means by which God, the sovereign Creator, maintains His power and authority. For this reason, the adversary seeks relentlessly to separate our children from the knowledge and acceptance of their sonship in God. His greatest reminder of his impending doom is the seed of woman. He dreads the allegiance and obedience of our righteous seed of promise.

You and I are literally battling for our sons and daughters, and for their children after them. They are the keys to God's redemption of the generations to come and the nations into which they are born. When God decided that it was time to deliver His seed, Israel, from the affliction and bondage of slavery under Egypt, His chosen vessel of deliverance was a child, a son. When Pharaoh saw the growing strength of the Jews, he was moved by a cunning and jealous Satan to target the children, the seed, the sons of Israel.

The focus of heaven and hell always centers on the children of destiny, the generation of hope.

Not only had God purposed to free His children, but He also staked the future of the children of Egypt on the obedience or disobedience of Pharaoh. When Pharaoh hardened his heart, when he refused to free God's chosen seed, then God sovereignly dealt him the most powerful blow any man can ever receive—the death of his firstborn. Once again, this was a battle for the seed.

Behold Your Seed!

As we survey our own era, with its affliction, bondage, and pain, we must search deep within our history for the generational links. Where can they be found? Where is the umbilical cord of our history? Did our fathers' fathers have to spill their blood for their own generation to survive? Did the sons of our ancestors have to pay the full price for our freedom in this generation? Did our mothers' mothers have to rear their children to perform the work of deliverers, prophets, priests, and kings on behalf of the generations that followed?

Why do we walk with head held high, with kingly stride, and with shoulders strong enough to bear the weight of government? Black man, why does your spirit refuse to be crushed, and why have you never broken under the pressure of injustice in your generation? African, Englishman, why are you so resilient when the pressures of nations and invaders threaten your homeland and your own sense of well-being? What sacrifices and vows have been made by your fathers to give you such an inheritance of freedom, hope, and vision?

Christian, how can you stand in the face of a godless culture gone wild with rebellion, sin, and despair? The answer is found in your foundations, and ultimately it is found in the Seed of David, the Messiah. It is found in the righteous seed born in the generations before you who faithfully bore the Savior's reproach and followed His footsteps from generation to generation, from the foot of the cross to the doors of our homes. This unbroken chain of the generations of righteous seed is God's vehicle of destiny.

We cannot shake off our history, because it brings not only shame, but also hope. The story of our generations brings not only pain, but also the promise of life. Sometimes it seems I can hear the mother of Moses whispering amidst the cries of the drowning sons of Israel:

Not this one! Not you, my child! For I discern in your eyes an infinite depth of my history.

I see within the depths of your striving a determination to live.

I see a future hope, a radically fierce determination to survive—for you must set your people free!

I can almost hear the heart of Joseph beating with excitement and wonder as he looks into the eyes of newborn Jesus:

Are You Mary's child? Whose Son are You?

Born to die, born to crush the head of Satan, born to set Your brothers free!

And so I will bear You in my arms and I will give You to Your Father and I will teach You who You are.

I will disciple You with servanthood, and You will learn to love Your people.

You will learn to obey Your heavenly Father and blindly to perform His bidding.

You will learn every promise purposed for You, and You will reach up into eternity and take hold of every word spoken of You.

You will say, "That the Scripture and the word of the prophets might be fulfilled, I go."

I, my Son, will stand aside and let You be about Your Father's business. And I will stand amazed as You bring judgment to Your generation and hope to all men of every race and of every age.

Then will I fully understand how God could invest His divine hope in such a Son as You...as He spoke to our fathers, to Abraham, and to his seed forever.

A Word for You

Are you a godly man or woman? Then you too must reproduce after your own kind—godly seed! You and I must follow the footsteps of Mary and humbly reply to the word of the Lord, *"Be it unto me according to thy word"* (Luke 1:38). You and I must pray and declare, "May my sons and daughters rise in their generation to crush the head of Satan!"

God is looking for righteous seed to assume the responsibility and dominion authority of prophets, priests, and kings in their generation. However, if you want to be a generational link, you must first learn some important lessons.

You must develop a strong sense of history and consider the purpose of your survival. God's purpose for you is to bring forth children of promise who have history locked up in their loins and whose spirits are injected with all the strength of their past. They have inherited the legacy of great kings, the fortitude of great warriors, the psalmistry of ancient minstrels, and the compassion of great prophets!

Raise your sons and daughters to run with the bravest, to survive with the strongest, and to reach for the highest call. Raise up your children to be the prophets, priests, and kings of their generation.

Learn God's purpose for your life and for your children's lives. Discover the eternal value of your decisions and collaborate with God for the salvation of the next generation. God clearly outlines His intended purpose for our righteous seed, and He provides a wealth of promises to help us fulfill our divine call to raise up righteous seed who will know the God of their fathers.

The Purpose of Our Seed

God created us with the ability to reproduce seed after our own kind because He has a very specific purpose for our race in the earth.

1. *To replenish the earth* (Gen. 1:28). The first purpose of our seed is to provide for the continuing work of God, who made us and commanded us to be fruitful and to replenish the earth. We are to do this by reproducing after our own kind, by having and rearing children made in God's image and likeness.
2. *To continue the dominion mandate* (Gen 1:28). God told Adam that he would have dominion over every other created thing. Thus, Adam was God's steward, responsible for keeping the garden and maintaining order and harmony. As a higher being, created in the image and likeness of God, man was a spirit invested with dominion authority. Each generation, reproduced after the image and likeness of their parents, will retain this authority. We must train our children to execute stewardship and dominion in the earth. Dominion is their destiny!
3. *To replicate God's image and likeness* (Gen. 1:26–28). What God started, He continues to do. Like the first man, and

those who followed him from generation to generation, our children are born with the image and likeness of God. That means our children have immense potential, as well as some qualities that are much like those of our heavenly Father.

4. *To inherit God's covenantal and eternal promises* (Isa. 59:21; Gen. 9:9, 12; 17:7–9, 15–19; 26:24; 28:13–14; Deut. 6:1–3). The eternal promises of the infinite God are to be received by all the generations of finite man's seed. This is God's way of extending His eternal promises from one lifetime to the next in the temporary world of man.
5. *To transmit God's law to the next generation* (Joel 1:3; Ps. 78:1–8). If God's kingdom is an everlasting kingdom that spans from generation to generation, then the role of the righteous seed is to pass on the message of God's kingdom and His law to the next generation.
6. *To be God's heritage and reward* (Ps. 127:3). God the Father perpetuates His fatherhood through the procreative work of godly parents who continually delight their Father God by presenting Him with more and more sons and daughters. (This does not negate the necessity of salvation by personal repentance and acceptance of Christ Jesus as Lord and Savior. It simply means a new generation is born and reared under the conscientious instruction and discipleship of God's Word by godly parents.)
7. *To still the enemy and the avenger* (Ps. 8:2). When children lift praises to God, they silence and still the avenger. Every generation of godly seed inherits the task of praising God in their generation and, by doing so, destroying the works of the enemy. Only eternity will reveal the tremendous and detrimental effect of children's perfect praise on the avenger.
8. *To deliver nations* (Judg. 13:5; Jer. 1:5–10). God is always looking for righteous seed who will rise up to be national

deliverers. The battle with Satan is for property and large-scale dominion.

9. *To inherit the earth* (Ps. 25:13; 69:35–36). We inherit responsibility by assuming the headship of a family or community. This means our seed is called to be the leaders and judges, the prophets, priests, and kings of their generation. They execute God's purposes while the masses rebel against God's laws.
10. *To be the substance of the earth* (Isa. 6:13). Substance means sustenance. When God sees our godly seed diligently holding forth His light and honoring His Word in the midst of their generation, He will show mercy and withhold His judgment from that generation.
11. *To proclaim God's faithfulness and show off God's blessi*ng (Isa. 61:9; Ps. 89:1; 102:18). This is the work of one generation to another. It guarantees that successive generations will not forget God's providence and goodness.
12. *To be accountable to God for their generation* (Ps. 22:30–31). When God sees the righteousness of the godly seed of a generation, He has mercy and grace for that whole generation.

Promises for Our Seed

God has given us a rich inheritance of promises in His Word. Many, if not most, of these promises are given for our children, His cherished righteous seed and torchbearers for the next generation. God's promises, given specifically for the next generation, include the following:

> *I will pour my spirit upon thy seed, and my blessing upon thine offspring.* (Isa. 44:3)

> *But the seed of the righteous shall be delivered.* (Prov. 11:21)

His seed [the man who fears the Lord] *shall be mighty upon earth: the generation of the upright shall be blessed.* (Ps. 112:2)

Thy seed will I establish for ever. (Ps. 89:4)

For God will save Zion, and will build the cities of Judah: that they may dwell there, and have it in possession. The seed also of his servants shall inherit it. (Ps. 69:35–36)

I [have] *not seen the righteous forsaken, nor his seed begging bread...and his seed is blessed.* (Ps. 37:25–26)

His seed [the man who fears the Lord] *shall inherit the earth.* (Ps. 25:13)

And all thy children shall be taught of the Lord*; and great shall be the peace of thy children.* (Isa. 54:13)

Strategies for the Preservation of Seed Who Will Lead

God's Word provides many examples of fathers and mothers who refused to stand by helplessly when situations, circumstances, or open attacks of the enemy threatened the welfare and destiny of their children. Here are some biblical ways we are exhorted to protect and direct our righteous seed:

1. Intercede and battle for your children using your spiritual weapons of warfare. In Genesis 3:15, God said that our seed will crush the head of Satan. By the principle of equivalent effect we are able to make this promise become ours today! Our seed will crush the enemy. If God has given you righteous seed, then He has made you able to intercede effectively for them.

2. Preserve the prophetic word spoken for each child. Utilize the principle of prophetic intention. This means that the word which is spoken out of the mouth of a parent for a

child will perform the purpose for which it was sent. Your child's prophetic purpose will preserve his very life! It is by this prophecy that your child can wage *"good warfare"* (1 Tim. 1:18).

3. Reproduce yourself. The principle of reproduction means that we will reproduce after our own kind! As you reproduce godly seed, you are ensuring their preservation as they inherit God's blessings.
4. Grow in your awareness of national problems facing your seed. Make every effort to discover and stop the enemy's diabolical plots and devices for their destruction (i.e. Planned "Parenthood," drugs, infidelity, perversion). Remain alert to Satan's plans to destroy your seed. Become articulate and active in your efforts.
5. Promote Christian education. Your seed is your best resource. Any educational system that does not have God at its center is methodically stealing your seed.
6. Think the way your generational, eternal God thinks. If you and I stop thinking about ourselves and turn our hearts to the children, God will activate blessings for us and for our seed.
7. Become "midwives" for your nation. The children of your entire nation are waiting for your intervention. It is a battle for the seed. If they are not claimed and brought into God's kingdom of light, they will be lost and destroyed in the kingdom of darkness.
8. Do not honor your children above God (1 Sam. 2:29–30). Eli the priest honored his sons above God, and God cursed his seed with early death. Restrain your seed from disobedience.
9. Show off God's faithfulness to your children (Ps. 71:18; 89:1–4). This empowers your children to expect and receive God's deliverance and blessing.

10. Strategize on behalf of your seed. Bathsheba strategized for her son Solomon to become king (1 Kings 1).

Preserve your child. Preserve God's prophetic word of promise for your child. Bathsheba had to remind aged King David that he had promised Solomon would be king. Speak up for your seed! Become alert and articulate, even to the point of being pushy if necessary!

You are the primary link between your children and the rich heritage of faith, godly wisdom, knowledge, and strength that you received in your own life through direct revelation and years of personal Bible study, as well as through parents, grandparents, mentors, teachers, and other spiritual leaders. Study to show yourself approved so you can rightly divide and model *"the word of truth"* before your righteous seed (2 Tim. 2:15).

3
The Power of Generational Thinking

How does finite man relate to an infinite eternity? How does a created being who is born, who lives and dies, relate with this vast eternity? How does one generation communicate values and time-tested principles to another generation? We can find the answers in studying the nature of God and in probing into the life histories of significant patriarchs.

How does God relate to us when He lives forever, but we live only a short time on the earth? How does God communicate to our generation of human beings and the generations that follow afterward? We can see the answer in nature and in His relationships with people in the Bible.

Our bodies offer us a powerful picture of God's plan for the generations. Every cell in the human body contains a deposit of information that confirm it belongs to a larger organism and that guides its individual development. That material, called DNA, is deposited at the heart of every cell.

Scientists have discovered that every human cell—whether it comes from a hair sample, a toenail clipping, blood or bone samples, or muscle tissue—contains a DNA strand that identifies it as part of one distinct human being. Additional information also appears in the strand that directs the specific function of specialized cells in such specialized organs as the liver, the eye, and the intestines.

Every human being begins his earthly existence by God's design and forethought as a pair of joined cells at conception. The first DNA strand is miraculously created at that point, and every cell in the body of a 180-pound man or a vivacious young woman grows from that tiny beginning and bears the same DNA "fingerprint" found in the first cells. The DNA is passed on or duplicated in every cell of our bodies throughout our lifetimes.

Jesus transformed an entire race by planting His "spiritual DNA" in other people. He spent three and a half years pouring His life into His disciples. When He ascended to heaven, He sealed the process by sending the Holy Spirit to dwell permanently in the hearts of His followers and changed the world forever.

When Jesus ascended, He intended for us to impact and change the generations of man in the same way. He wants you and I to plant spiritual DNA in the hearts of our children and instruct them to pass this legacy on to their children. We are to take this Gospel, this spiritual DNA, into all the world. But since God makes it clear that He considers our children to be His heritage, then our children must be our first mission field! God expects us to be good stewards of the treasures He has placed in our care.

The key we need in order to unlock the hearts of people today and of future generations lives, eats, and sleeps in our own homes—it is our children!

Jewish history tells us of how God especially honored, blessed, and trusted Abraham because he faithfully trained his children in the ways of God. God said this of him:

For I know him, that he will command his children and his household after him, and they shall keep the way of the LORD, to do justice and judgment; that the LORD may bring upon Abraham that which he hath spoken of him. (Gen. 18:19)

This Scripture passage perfectly demonstrates the concept of generations in action. It is this kind of dedicated mentoring, training, and discipling that has allowed the Jews to maintain a distinct identity and personality throughout centuries of persecution, dispersion, and suffering. The "DNA" of their heritage has been passed on from generation to generation.

Now is the time for us to pass the torch of our faith and vision to our future generations. God's command to the Israelites in Deuteronomy 6 still rings true for us today:

And thou shalt teach them [God's commandments, statutes, and judgments] *diligently unto thy children, and shalt talk of them when thou sittest in thine house, and when thou walkest by the way, and when thou liest down, and when thou risest up.* (Deut. 6:7)

Your understanding of the concept of generations hinges directly on your concept of God and His nature. How you receive this book relates directly to how you answer these questions:

1. What is the nature of God?
2. Who is God? How does He interact with man?
3. What is the nature of God's creation?

My understanding of our generational God is based on a foundation of significant truths. The sovereign God of creation is an eternal God. Therefore, everything He does is done with eternity in mind. God is not a short-term thinker.

God is self-existent; He does not require assistance or an external power source. He is infinite, without limits or measure. He has always existed; He has no beginning. He is Being itself. When He wants to do a thing, He possesses all the resources, power, knowledge, and ability to do it within Himself. However, in most cases, He chooses to use us.

God's nature encompasses and surpasses all time. God is bigger than time itself. He defines and encompasses all of the future and extends beyond all measurable time, even into the measureless reaches of eternity. When He tells us to do a thing, our response will affect all of eternity (even if we think it will be forgotten by the weekend).

Everything outside of God is a created thing. Every created thing has a measure, or fingerprint, of God's eternal nature—even the insects whose life spans are measured in minutes or hours. Nature is infiltrated, or infused, with the very essence of God. It is sustained solely by His will. Whatever God creates comes out of His being; therefore, it has divine proportions or dimensions.

God created our world according to His nature, so it runs and operates according to some basic laws that reflect His being. These laws affect our lives, the lives of our children, and the lives of their children after them.

The Law of Reproduction

God the Creator placed an inner drive, a natural instinct, within all living created things to continue the life that God placed within them. This divine instinct is the law of reproduction.

This law first appears in the first chapter of Genesis, the "Book of Beginnings":

And God said, Let the earth bring forth grass, the herb yielding seed, and the fruit tree yielding fruit after his

> *kind, whose seed is in itself, upon the earth: and it was so. And the earth brought forth grass, and herb yielding seed after his kind, and the tree yielding fruit, whose seed was in itself, after his kind: and God saw that it was good.*
> (Gen. 1:11–12)

The Creator specifically mentioned herbs, fruits, and seed in these verses. He said:

1. The created herb would be able to recreate itself or reproduce itself.
2. It would have seed within itself.
3. The seed produced would in turn produce fruit exactly like the fruit from which it came.

Two key features of this absolute natural law are significant: (1) Every created living thing (such as an apple tree) will produce fruit that has seeds within it, and (2) those seeds will always produce like kind. In the case of our example, apple seeds will always produce other apple trees.

The Eternal Nature of God's Purposes

When God creates or initiates something new, He places a measure or trace of His sustaining life within it. No life can exist apart from Him who is Life itself.

For purposes of expansion and reproduction, God also places within every created thing the ability and instinct to reproduce itself so He does not have to keep creating it anew. For instance, God does not have to keep speaking to the water to bring forth fish.

Every creative word spoken by God continues to operate over time and continues to accomplish the work for which it was sent forth. The power of God's spoken word, fueled by the power of God's divine intention, continues to obey the God of that word. This is the very nature of the law of creation.

The Law of Purpose

The divine law of purpose is that essence of determinism and directionality with which the thing manufactured or created is made. Long before the thing was created or born, there existed the need for which the thing was shaped. And even before the need existed, there was an even greater law of creation and perfection at work. This law moves all things toward restoration of originally intended perfection.

So, prior to a child's birth, a gigantic moving together of forces is initiated, impelled by a spirit of purpose and destiny, which pulls together that child with the life goal for which he will be born. This phenomenon of purpose and destiny joins together the beginning with the end for which it was created. Purpose impels, and destiny draws to itself the culmination, or fulfillment, of predetermined intention.

The Law of Creation

The law of creation is always in effect. Once a thing or function is instituted by the Creator, the power of God that brought the thing into being continues its life-giving, energizing work. The earth continues to produce plants because of that first eternal word of God, not because we dump tons of fertilizer and chemical additives on the soil every year.

According to Genesis 1:31, God was satisfied that He had made everything just as He had intended and that each created thing would do the work for which it was created. The divine law operating within creation would continue, and each created living thing would continue to regenerate itself by the divine thrust of the first word spoken by God.

The Reproduction of God's Image

God specially commanded the law of reproduction to operate when He created one creature above all others, the creature called Adam, who was created in His own image and likeness.

1. The first man, Adam, was created with the ability to reproduce himself through union with Eve. His offspring would have the same attributes with which he was first created.
2. Adam not only reproduced himself after his own kind, but union with Eve also produced seed that would mature and reproduce more of its kind because God ordained that each offspring would have the seeds within them to continue the reproductive process.

The book of Genesis says that Adam was created in the image and likeness of God (Gen. 1:26–27). Before the fall, Adam and Eve were evidently created to live forever, totally untouched by death or degeneration. At this point, the chief value of reproduction would have been to multiply, since the new race of man appeared to be in no danger of dying out. Adam and Eve did sin, though, and the need for reproduction became vitally important to man.

After a disappointing start with Cain and Abel, Adam and Eve had a son named Seth who was born in the image and likeness of his father, Adam (Gen. 5:3). This means that Seth was made in the image and likeness of God, like his father before him. In a very real sense, God continually reproduces men "after His own kind" (or image) with every child born on this planet.

The Purpose of Reproduction

The purpose of reproduction is to preserve and perpetuate the continuity of God's eternal purposes among the short-lived, temporal people who inhabit His created world. God is eternal. He has put into place all that is needed for continuity, or unbroken progress from generation to generation. Our eternal God has eternal dimensions. He is infinite and limitless, but He created living creatures, including man, to operate within the dimension of time.

Man's earthly existence is finite. It has a definite beginning and a definite end. For this reason, God deals with man in generational dimensions. For Infinity to execute His infinite purposes in and through finite creatures, the created must have the potential to recreate and reproduce itself.

When God dealt with Adam, He looked beyond the creature He formed with His hands. He saw the seed within Adam, and He saw the succeeding generations of seed that would follow.

The Promise, Seed, Generations, and Time

Adam and Eve transgressed God's law when they ate of the forbidden fruit. They were warned that *"in the day that thou eatest thereof thou shalt surely die"* (Gen. 2:17). Because they chose disobedience, Adam and Eve earned the wages of sin, which was death. Since the first Adam and his wife had become finite, limited creatures with a limited life span, the seed they produced would also be born to die.

Even when sin invades the hearts and lives of His created beings, God's purposes will not be set aside. Even before Adam's sin, the all-knowing God had already devised a plan to redeem the entire race of man. It began with the promise in Genesis 3:15:

> *And I will put enmity between thee and the woman, and between thy seed and her seed; it shall bruise thy head, and thou shalt bruise his heel.*

This promise held several presuppositions that have eternal consequences:

1. The woman would reproduce.
2. That seed, or that seed's seed, would be born with a specific purpose.

3. That purpose would be to bruise (crush) the head of Satan.

The wonderful promise held within it a ray of hope: the prospect that God's plan of deliverance would make good of what was bad. However, this promise of seed and succeeding generations had a futuristic dimension that would require time. Thus, time was initiated by God as the period within which man would restore a lost position. Until the fall of Adam and Eve, the only purpose for time was to measure night and day, for the race of man was created fully mature and experienced the passage of time without fear of death or aging. After the fall, however, every new day of existence brought new changes and signs of deterioration.

The first purpose of the generations was to ensure that a Messiah, who would completely destroy the power of the enemy and the sting of death, would enter the world in the *"fullness of time"* (1 Cor. 15:55). The second purpose of the generations is to bring God's life and light into the dark world of lost men from generation to generation. This purpose can only be fulfilled by spiritual "descendants" of the Second Adam, those who have received Jesus Christ as Lord and Savior. As recreated sons and daughters of God, reborn in the image and likeness of our Savior, we share our Lord's mission, commission, and authority in the earth. That is why we are literally His body on earth.

It is not difficult to imagine the despair Adam and Eve felt as they acknowledged their disobedience to God and awaited God's judgment. It is also easy to understand their gratitude for God's promise and their eager anticipation of its fulfillment.

God's promise required them to look within themselves for its fulfillment. God had said they would bring forth a seed that would bruise Satan's head. From that moment forward, the primary objective or expectation of Adam and Eve was to eagerly await the birth of the seed. Eve expressed this in Genesis 4:1 when she gave birth to the first human baby in history: *"And Adam knew Eve his wife; and she conceived, and bare Cain, and said, I have gotten a man from the LORD."*

I believe the birth of Cain, followed by that of Abel, brought a short-lived hope to their parents: "Which one would be the deliverer-seed?" The hope of these first parents must have been shaken when their first son became earth's first murderer, and their second son its first murder victim. In her joy over her third son's conception and birth, Eve named him Seth, which means, appropriately, "appointed." *"For God, said she, hath appointed me another seed instead of Abel, whom Cain slew"* (Gen. 4:25).

Seth was an "appointed" seed, earmarked for the fulfillment of the grand promise of God the Father: "You will have a seed." The prophet Isaiah told us that God's ways are above man's (Isa. 55:9). It may also be true to say that God's concept of time is different from ours. *"But, beloved, be not ignorant of this one thing, that one day is with the Lord as a thousand years, and a thousand years as one day"* (2 Pet. 3:8).

The eternal God looks on our world from a position of eternity where there is an everlasting dimension. God cannot be contained by time, nor by its limited dimension. He simply is not bound by its proportions or its limits. God sees and regards man from an eternal "pre-fall dimension," where man was created for God's eternal fellowship and enjoyment. He sees us as He intends for us to be. He has also given us the ability to stretch out our existence beyond our own lifetimes, into our succeeding generations.

God sees the seed within man and it is accounted unto Him for man's continuity. The eternal God operates with man in eternal dimensions, eternal promises, an eternal Word, and eternal covenants. God created man with an eternal dimension in two realms: Each human being possesses a living *spirit* that never dies, and each has a living *body* with a soul that extends its life on earth by reproducing seed after its own kind.

When God looks at a man or a woman, He sees the promise of seed and the hope of generations, a seed with the potential to continue its preordained purpose to crush Satan's head.

The Law of Equivalent Effect

Ever since the first human baby entered the world, generation after generation has been born with divine imperative and precision. Every person born on this planet was born with a calling and a promise for the fulfillment of purpose. Each woman's womb was prepared over and over again for the conception of the promised seed.

Since the birth of Adam and Eve's first son, the human race has marked the birth of seed as a pivotal event. The birth of seed signaled the survival of the family and the thrust of one generation into lives of future generations.

> *This is the book of the generations of Adam. In the day that God created man, in the likeness of God made he him....and Adam lived an hundred and thirty years, and begat a son in his own likeness, after his image; and called his name Seth: and the days of Adam after he had begotten Seth were eight hundred years: and he begat sons and daughters.*
> (Gen. 5:1, 3–4)

Each generation held hope and promise. Every man and woman in the genealogical line of Jesus the Messiah made a unique and preordained contribution to the fulfillment of God's ancient promise.

When God's Word is spoken, it begins and continues to perform the work for which it was created. *"So shall my word be that goeth forth out of my mouth: it shall not return unto me void, but it shall accomplish that which I please, and it shall prosper in the thing whereto I sent it"* (Isa. 55:11).

Each succeeding generational link performs its task and completes a part, not the whole, of God's eternal purpose. Abraham had to see himself as part of that generational chain. He had to project himself into the future because the promise God gave him had future dimensions.

1. The promise was for seed.
2. The seeds of promise would perform mighty works for God.
3. Abraham could only receive promises for his own lifetime, based on the condition that he would anticipate seed, reproduce seed, and teach that seed obedience to God's law (Gen. 18:17–19). The part of the promise destined to be fulfilled in a future generation could only be perceived and received by faith.

God's promise to Abraham was wrapped up in Abraham's seed, so Abraham had to become a generational man. He had to begin to think the way God thinks, for when the eternal God looks at a man, He sees more than just the man—He sees the man and his seed, stretching from the man's present far into his future.

God is willing to make a covenant with any man or woman who has this eternal dimension. An eternal covenant can only be received by a man who has ceased to see himself as bound by time. That man must stretch himself into God's eternal present and God's immeasurable and unlimited future by producing seed and generations of seed, the seeds of eternal promise!

The Example of Noah

Did Noah stumble on God's purpose for him and his seed? Noah (whose name means "rest" or "comfort") was born ten generations after Adam. By that time, God the Father and Creator had perceived that the created world was quickly becoming overrun by the work of the enemy, Satan. *"Every imagination of the thoughts of* [man's] *heart was only evil continually. And it repented the LORD that he had made man"* (Gen. 6:5–6).

God had a dream, and man's purpose was to fulfill God's dream. It seemed that the entire race was on a path to destruction, but God knew that He only needed one man and his seed in order to crush the head of the enemy.

God searched the earth and found one man who possessed all that was necessary to preserve God's plan for future generations. Noah was found to be *"perfect in his generations"* (Gen. 6:9). He also had three sons and their wives. This was a perfect scenario for the performance of God's purpose in generations to come, *"to keep seed alive upon the face of all the earth"* (Gen. 7:3).

God had devised a plan to preserve a remnant from every seed-bearing living creature that could not survive the coming deluge. All of His creatures, including Noah and his children, were invested with the responsibility to preserve their seed through God's laws of creation and reproduction. It was crucial to God's plan that Noah's sons and their wives obey Noah's call to enter the ark.

After the flood, recorded in Genesis 7, God repeated to Noah His Edenic covenant promise for reproduction and multiplication. Once again, the divine prospect of the Deliverer-Seed underlay the covenant promise of God to man. He was determined to redeem this race of spirit creatures He had made.

The law of equivalent effect states that "every generational man (male or female) must see himself as a generational link in the plan of God for the salvation of the world."

1. He must hear the words spoken by God in the promise given in Genesis 3:15.

2. That word must be heard as it was first spoken.
3. It must be appropriated by the hearer in a subsequent generation as if it were spoken for him.
4. That hearer must say as Mary did, *"Be it unto me according to thy word"* (Luke 1:38).

The key to our fulfillment of purpose as Christians, and as created living creatures, is this: We must be willing to produce seeds of promise for our generation, and for the next.

God's Modus Operandi

We need to understand how important and how central this concept of generations is to God's purposes on the earth. Ask yourself, "How does an infinite, eternal, covenant God interact with finite, mortal man? How does a Father God provide for His children?"

The only answer to this question is "through the generations." God intended to redeem our race through His own Seed, but He needed a "vineyard of flesh" in which to plant Himself. First, He preserved a remnant through Noah and his descendants. Then He chose to honor His servant from a later generation, Abraham, by setting apart his seed as the earthly vehicle to deliver God's Deliverer-Seed, Jesus Christ.

God chose to work through generations, and through the seed of woman, time and again because the concepts of generations and seed are His ideas. Is it so surprising that He wants to work through our seed as well?

The purposes, laws, and statutes of God are eternal, so many of them can only be obeyed or realized through succeeding generations. Nearly every type and symbol in the old and new covenants reflect this eternal aspect of His nature. The incense that was burned upon the ark was to be *"a perpetual incense before the LORD throughout your generation"* (Exod. 30:8).

Under the old covenant, the sacrificial offering for atonement would be made yearly, but it was to have a continuous effect. God said that the atonement was to be made *"once in a year...**throughout your generations**"* (Exod. 30:10, emphasis added). Sabbaths were to be observed by Israel *"throughout their generations, for a perpetual covenant"* (Exod. 31:16).

For unbroken priestly service and for God's blessing to flow to the people perpetually, God had to choose a father and his son to create a tribe or class of priests who would be solely devoted to their priestly service (Exod. 27:21; 28:1).

The Everlasting Priesthood

God's goal was to raise up a nation, an everlasting generation of priests unto His name. Adam and Eve were truly priests who represented the Creator to His created world, especially to the creatures of the Garden of Eden. That priesthood was profaned and ended prematurely by sin. The end of the first man's perfect relationship with God and his entry into temporal life with its final earthly ending in death forever changed life on earth. This necessitated sanctification, separation, and anointing of entire generations of new children. It also demanded a transgenerational selection of children to take the priestly responsibility of fathers to their respective generations.

Responsibility of Fathers

This priesthood demands not only a life of purity, duty, and ministry of fathers, but also the strict training and discipleship of children to do likewise. Fathers were held personally responsible to hand down to their children three important priestly ordinances ordained by God:

1. They were to keep their seed pure. *"Neither shall he profane his seed among his people: for I the LORD do sanctify him"* (Lev. 21:15).

2. The priests were continually warned of God's swift hand of judgment. *"Speak unto Aaron and to his sons, that they separate themselves...that they profane not my holy name....Say unto them, Whosoever he be of all your seed among your generations...having his uncleanness upon him, that soul shall be cut off from my presence: I am the LORD"* (Lev. 22:2–3).
3. The priests were expected to restrain and rebuke their children. Failure to do so would mean God's judgment.

God meant everything He said about His requirements for the priesthood. Two very different priests in the Bible experienced catastrophic failure in their lives because of their sons.

Aaron's sons learned the exact specifications and guidelines for their priestly service from their father, yet they still offered *"strange fire"* before the Lord (Lev. 10:1). Perhaps they were simply following in their father's footsteps, once again making a "golden calf" for a new generation that did not know God (Exod. 32:1–7). Regardless of their reasons, God's judgment was swift. Fire came from heaven and devoured them. It is interesting to see that God forbade Aaron to grieve for his dead sons when they were chastised by Him (Lev. 10:6).

Generations later, another high priest in Aaron's order failed to restrain his sons and paid a heavy price. Eli allowed his sons to defiantly and publicly engage in lascivious and sacrilegious behavior. The Bible literally says he honored his sons above God (1 Sam. 2:29)! Again, God moved to maintain the purity of the priesthood and the glory of His presence. *"Behold, the days come, that I will cut off thine arm, and the arm of thy father's house, that there shall not be an old man in thine house"* (1 Sam. 2:31).

In the book of Malachi, God spoke to the priests and repeated His warning. If the priests continued to break family covenants by their unfaithfulness, then God would corrupt their seed (Mal. 2:3). God desires godly seed (Mal. 2:15), and His desire has not changed since the Garden of Eden. He longs for sons and daughters, for godly seed who will be faithful to Him from generation to generation. He wants to raise up generational priests who see beyond the limited years of their own lifetimes, to see in the spirit the unbroken generations of their seed proclaiming God's praises.

As always, the responsibility rests in our hands, for God has finished His work and placed it at our disposal. All we need are willing hearts, sensitive ears, and courage—all of which are fueled by the power of generational thinking!

4

Train Your Children for the Priesthood

Time-tested principles governing moral codes must be passed on from generation to generation. The laws and ordinances governing nations must be learned and obeyed by one generation and taught by that generation to the next.

Within every society, specific individuals have been given the vocational call and special graces and giftedness to be the spiritual teachers and guides to the people. These are the persons who have been called to become the priests, counselors, rabbis, or mentors of their communities.

In Jewish tradition and history, the firstborn child has been set apart as the one who would receive the firstborn inheritance and blessing. There is a specific claim on the firstborn. He would receive the greater portion, that is two-thirds, of the financial inheritance and of land and other resources. But with that legacy came the responsibility for the other surviving parent, stewardship of the family business, and care of the household and property. The paramount role of the inheritor of firstborn blessings was to bear another firstborn son who would bear the family name and would be the successor and inheritor of family property.

The child who first "opened" the womb was also considered the one who lifted the shame of barrenness from the woman and ushered in the blessings ordained for that family.

The history of the Jewish nation contains the masterstroke of God, designed by Him for the progressive and continued restoration of men and nations back to godly living.

At one pivotal moment in their history God had to make this declaration:

> *Because all the firstborn are mine; for on the day that I smote all the firstborn in the land of Egypt I hallowed unto me all the firstborn in Israel, both man and beast: mine shall they be: I am the LORD.* (Num. 3:13)

Why did God demand the firstborn and claim them as His own? What of the second- and third-born; can they too be given to God?

God the Father said to the Son and the Holy Spirit, *"Let us make man in our image"* (Gen. 1:26). Adam was created out of the covenant love and agreement of the Father, Son, and Holy Spirit. God's life-giving word still continues to operate in Adam's distant descendants through the reproduction and procreation process. So our Father God still continues to give life and birth to His children.

God is vitally concerned with each generation's task of representing Him on the earth. The children of God assume the roles of prophet, priest, and king, thus performing service to God on behalf of men. By claiming the firstborn as His own, God has:

1. Ensured the execution of prophetic, priestly, and kingly services on the earth.

2. Secured the services of the child to whom belonged the double portion of the father's inheritance and blessing under ancient Jewish tradition.
3. Procured and ensured the services of every family member by claiming the service of one.
4. Selected one through whom generations of seed would come so the Messiah, God's only begotten Son, would be born. The seed would remain pure, earmarked for priestly service.
5. Gained the worship of the entire family through the one.
6. Ensured that fathers who willingly trained their firstborn to assume God-given responsibilities would reap the benefits of that child's service. The father would, in turn, give the rest of his children to God's service. In other words, "If you've got the firstborn, you will most likely get the whole tribe." God is a God of wisdom, and He is also a God of divine economy. His actions are to be perceived from a broad, long-range, and eternal perspective. If a father is willing to give up his firstborn to God, he most likely will be willing to give God the rest.
7. Carefully instructed the Hebrews concerning the responsibility of the firstborn. He knew that a child, particularly a son, who was trained to receive the total responsibility for his family if his father died, would be the one who could receive and accommodate additional priestly and prophetic responsibilities.

Under the new covenant, ratified by the blood of Jesus Christ, we are all kings and priests. God no longer simply seeks the first fruits, the firstborn, or the tithe—He demands all that we are, all that we have, and all that we hope to be. What then can we learn about raising "firstborn sons"? The answer is that all of our children are called and anointed to represent God in their generation! They are all worthy and chosen to receive the blessings of the firstborn in Christ. They must all be taught to assume the responsibilities and duties of leadership in their lives.

The priests in the Bible did not always live up to their responsibilities. They often broke God's law and caused their children to break God's law and family covenants. The problem became so widespread that God was not being properly served and represented by the firstborn of the families. Finally, He set apart a tribe of priests who would themselves reproduce priests (Num. 3:45). God's selection of the tribe of Levi is a type and shadow of the greater spiritual reality that was revealed when God sent His only Son to establish a spiritual nation of priests.

Now, we and our children are all made to be kings and priests, to assume the office of the firstborn on behalf of the nations, and to pass on those blessings and responsibilities to our own children.

> *To the general assembly and church of the firstborn, which are written in heaven, and to God the Judge of all, and to the spirits of just men made perfect.* (Heb. 12:23)

> *For whom he did foreknow, he also did predestinate to be conformed to the image of his Son, that he might be the firstborn among many brethren.* (Rom. 8:29)

> *And hath made us kings and priests unto God and his Father; to him be glory and dominion for ever and ever. Amen.* (Rev. 1:6)

When Jesus atoned for man's sin through His death and resurrection, He became the firstborn of many sons, and thus, by spiritual procreation, He raised up for Himself an everlasting generation of firstborn, who are heirs and joint-heirs with Him (Rom. 8:17).

We are a kingdom of priests unto God, a holy nation, the new covenant fulfillment of the Levitical type and shadow.

The Old Covenant Type and Shadow

> *Now therefore, if ye will obey my voice indeed, and keep my covenant, then ye shall be a peculiar treasure unto me above all people: for all the earth is mine: and ye shall be unto me a kingdom of priests, and an holy nation. These are the words which thou shalt speak unto the children of Israel.*
> (Exod. 19:5–6)

The New Covenant Fulfillment in Grace

> *Ye also, as lively stones, are built up a spiritual house, an holy priesthood, to offer up spiritual sacrifices, acceptable to God by Jesus Christ....But ye are a chosen generation, a royal priesthood, an holy nation, a peculiar people; that ye should show forth the praises of him who hath called you out of darkness into his marvellous light.* (1 Pet. 2:5, 9)

Our sons and daughters are priests, kings, and prophets. Once they personally receive Jesus Christ as Lord and Savior, they become members of the assembly of the firstborn (Heb. 12:23). They are sanctified and anointed by God for firstborn blessings and responsibilities.

God selected Abraham to raise up a nation by faith through his promised seed. That nation was to be an example to other nations; a holy nation whose obedience to God's law would restrain His hand of wrath from their neighbors and who would ultimately produce a delivering Seed.

God still places this responsibility upon His spiritual nation, the church. Every generation in the church is to be the sustenance, the seed counted unto the Lord for a generation (Ps. 22:30).

It is the responsibility of Christian parents to consecrate every child to the service of God. As prophets, priests, and kings, our children are destined to evangelize and discipline the nations and to assume governmental responsibilities in every sphere of life.

When Sons Lose the Firstborn's Blessings

This responsibility to raise up priests and kings in our homes is extremely important to our Maker. He has a vested interest in the seed, and He holds us directly responsible for our stewardship of our children. One example of a man's firstborn child breaking God's law and losing his inheritance serves as a solemn warning to us in our day. If a firstborn son proves unreliable, unwise, or unwilling to accept the responsibility of leadership, godly parents are to carefully determine which child or children deserve and want to receive the inheritance.

> *Now the sons of Reuben the firstborn of Israel, (for he was the firstborn; but, forasmuch as he defiled his father's bed, his birthright was given unto the sons of Joseph the son of Israel: and the genealogy is not to be reckoned after the birthright. For Judah prevailed above his brethren, and of him came the chief ruler; but the birthright was Joseph's.)*
> (1 Chron. 5:1–2)

> *Reuben, thou art my firstborn, my might, and the beginning of my strength, the excellency of dignity, and the excellency of power: unstable as water, thou shalt not excel; because thou wentest up to thy father's bed; then defiledst thou it: he went up to my couch.* (Gen. 49:3–4)

Jacob's firstborn son, Reuben, was not given first place or prominence in the genealogy of Jacob's sons because of his sin. The Bible record literally breaks off the narrative on genealogy to comment on how God handled the sin of this firstborn son of Jacob and Leah. Sin matters to God. Because of sin, He chose to revoke His own order that established the firstborn as legal heir to the birthright.

Reuben forfeited two rights when he lay with his father's concubine and brought dishonor to the whole family. First, the royal seed, the promised Messiah, would not descend through Reuben, but through the seed of his younger brother, Judah. Second, Reuben lost the firstborn's privilege and responsibility of financially caring for his father and his younger brothers. That honor later went to Joseph. It was also Joseph's seed, Ephraim and Manasseh, who arose as heads of two of the twelve tribes in place of Reuben and Simeon (whom God had originally intended to be set apart).

Our children must be informed of who they are in Christ and of their prophetic, priestly, and kingly roles in their nation and to their generation.

The truth is that the genealogy of God's kingdom is based on a higher law than natural birthright. The genealogies, the birth of children, and the generational lineage from which the Messiah came were not automatic. God's working out of generational blessings does not take place simply because a child is born. It is God who directs the giftings of children. It is He who, at times, overrules natural inheritance to choose children of destiny (such as David and Joseph).

God does not choose children who, like Reuben, are as "*unstable as water*" (Gen. 49:4). God looks at the heart of each child to see if there is the potential and the will to be a prophet, priest, or king. Where God finds a child lacking, He looks to another, at least until another day when—as with John Mark, who became a favored "son" to the apostle Paul even after he had failed Paul and been rejected for ministry work once before—a second chance is offered. The natural firstborn does have rights, but some have not been found worthy. Jacob's heart was broken as he offered only a partial blessing on Reuben, his fallen firstborn son who had such potential for dignity, excellence, and power.

> *Reuben, thou art my firstborn, my might, and the beginning of my strength, the excellency of dignity, and the excellency of power: unstable as water, thou shalt not excel; because thou wentest up to thy father's bed; then defiledst thou it: he went up to my couch.* (Gen. 49:3–4)

What indescribable sadness did Jacob feel as he uttered these prophetic words and looked into the second-rate future of his firstborn? And what of you and me? When we look into the hearts of our children, what do we see? Do we see strength, grace, and beauty? Do we see potential for excellence and honor?

Do we share Jacob's pain as we detect instability, weakness of character, lack of motivation, an unwillingness to assume responsibility, or a careless indifference to parental approval along with a lukewarm desire for God's approval? You and I must consider our situation and do whatever we must to redeem our seed!

I search the eyes, the hearts, and the souls of my children.

I probe eagerly and deeply into their spirits

And I look for the little flicker, I look for that little flame,

That flame of glory passed on by divine inheritance.

I look to see the strength of that flame.

And gently I fan the flame, as I wipe away the tears of disappointment.

Gently I remove the embers—they must not block the life-giving air. My child must breathe deeply of the call of God upon his life.

Gently I blow the breath of my love, and with that breath goes my prayer.

"Be it done unto me according to Thy word,

"Lord, You promised...my child, my firstborn child..."

And lovingly I gather him in my arms and gently, gently whisper.

I whisper the prophetic words he's heard so often,

I whisper my own promise, plea, and oath.

And with my whisper goes the power of love, the strength of a parent's blessing!

And that power quickly gathers up the hopes and fears of his fathers' God, and the cry of the waiting world;

And the still uncut umbilical cord of a priestly, kingly, and prophetic father, and the fervent hope of an anguished mother.

And out of the cinders like a brilliant flame arises my child's strong call.

Crushing cankerworm and palmerworm,

Redeeming the lost years,

And moving swiftly to obedience,

My child receives his true inheritance!

How to Bless Your Children: The Meaning of a Blessing

One of the most important abilities parents have in Christ is the ability to bless their children. The concept of blessing someone is a biblical one that has the added authority given by the "principle of first mention." If we ask when this word was first used in God's Word, we find that it was one of the first terms used by God in relation to children! What does it mean to bless your children?

1. *To bless means to "give a gift to."* The first use of the word often translated as "*bless*" appears in Genesis 1:22, where God gave to all living creatures the gifts of fruitfulness, multiplication, and the right to occupy the whole earth.

The second blessing was the power of procreation mentioned in Genesis 1:28, where God repeated to man the gift of increase and occupancy of the earth. It was a blessing that would guarantee the birth and procreation of seed of destiny on the earth.

The third blessing was just as significant as that of reproduction. God also gave man the blessing of dominion and rulership over all other creatures—the beasts, the birds, and the fish (Gen. 1:26–28; Ps. 8). This blessing guaranteed the rise of generations of godly seed who would be the leaders of their generation. They would be children of dominion!

2. *A blessing is a good gift bestowed upon another.* God (who sees the end from the beginning and who is a God of long-term vision and purpose) blessed man with gifts He knew that men would need.

   After man's fall, God's blessing of procreation was the only way for Eve to bring forth a seed destined to bruise the head of Satan. Fruitfulness in childbearing was a blessing and the only way to bring forth a redeemer. To be barren was therefore a curse!

   After the Flood, the blessing of reproduction was again Noah's only way to realize the fulfillment of God's covenant promise in Genesis 9:1. This time God added another dimension to His blessing when He told Noah and his children: *"Be fruitful, and multiply, and replenish the earth. And the fear of you and the dread of you shall be upon every beast of the earth, and upon every fowl...into your hand are they delivered"* (Gen. 9:1–2). All animals have a fear of man, and this protects man's natural dominion.

   God had already created and formed man's body with its built-in capacity for reproduction. However, the pronouncement of the blessing released that capability in man.

3. *A blessing releases natural abilities.* A blessing releases supernatural dominion ability. It is a *transgenerational* means of procuring God's gifts. The next mention of blessing appears when God calls Abram to leave Ur of the Chaldees and go into Canaan.

   And I will make of thee a great nation, and I will bless thee, and make thy name great; and thou shalt be a blessing: and I will bless them that bless thee, and curse him that curseth thee: and in thee shall all families of the earth be blessed. (Gen. 12:2–3).

   In this case, *"To bless"* means to multiply your seed and to be made to have a great name. It also means that the blessed one is protected from the curses of others. It means that, by the blessing of one, many more will receive blessing.

   This type of blessing is received only by those who think long-term, generationally, and optimistically. It is received only by those who are willing to submit to the eternal, unchanging, and sometimes painful covenant of a covenant-keeping God.

   This kind of blessing is spoken by those who sense a parental responsibility to pass on a blessing. The blessing of children foretells the history of nations and ensures rulership and prosperity.

   Another significant mention of blessing is found in chapters 48 and 49 of Genesis, where Jacob called his sons and grandsons and blessed them. This blessing strongly implies that the one blessed would receive the gifts and responsibilities needed for the future survival of a nation. The one who is blessed must carry on the generational call of bringing forth a nation for God.

   It furthermore established God's *modus operandi* and the pattern He has passed on to us. Parents and grandparents are given the ability and responsibility to bless children and grandchildren.

4. *A "paternal blessing" is a father's blessing to a son or daughter who must bear the responsibility of* ***generational leadership****.* Joseph tried to place the patriarch Jacob's right hand on the head of the firstborn son, but Jacob instead granted the paternal blessing to the second-born son, Ephraim (Gen. 48:8–20).

   It is clear that God has given to godly parents and grandparents the prophetic and foretelling abilities to bless (or to curse) our children.

   This blessing for both of Joseph's sons has a very special significance. The blessing was for the sons who would be the heads of two of the twelve tribes of Israel. It endued these *grandsons* with the rights and privileges of *sons.* In Genesis 48:5, Jacob claimed his grandsons as his sons, destined to be part of the great nation that was promised him by God. Ephraim was to take the place of Reuben, and Manasseh, the place of Simeon.

   The firstborn's blessing, given to the younger son, Ephraim, held significance. It was out of his lineage that the Savior-Seed would now come.

5. *The blessing of a seed procures fulfillment of God's promise and ensures the generational activity of God among a people.* Genesis 49:28 says that Jacob blessed his sons *"according to his blessing."* That means he spoke prophetically into their lives. He said, *"Gather yourselves together, that I may tell you that which shall befall you in the last days"* (Gen. 49:1).

   The deportment and behavior of sons of a nation determines the life and history of that nation. Communities and nations are shaped by the cultures men develop.

6. *The blessing of children proclaims a prophetic word for the future of men and nations.* Jacob's blessing over his sons had three significant purposes:

   a. *A father's blessing places and calls forth specific* ***rulership ability*** *in his children and his children's children.* A blessing sets apart those who are ordained to have significant positions of authority. Jacob prophesied that the scepter (signifying the authority of rulership) would not depart from *Judah's* line (Gen. 49:10). The Messiah would come from the tribe of Judah. Jacob also said that God would bless *Joseph* and his seed. Ephraim, Joseph's son, later ruled one of the strongest tribes.

   b. *A father's blessing activates success, prosperity, and creativity in his children.* The paternal blessing of Jacob released gifts upon his sons that they would need for survival. Zebulun, for example, received special trading ability, and Judah and Asher received material prosperity. Naphtali received the gift of the *"goodly words"* (Gen. 49:21) of poetry and prose.

   c. *A paternal blessing overrules every other blessing and every curse spoken over the seed.* A father's blessing prevails above the blessings (or curses!) of siblings and others. These blessings are expansive and endure forever. Joseph was rejected by his brothers and sold into cruel slavery, but Jacob said, *"The blessings of thy father have prevailed above the blessings of my progenitors unto the utmost bound of the everlasting hills"* (Gen. 49:26).

The following important lessons can be learned from the biblical examples of paternal blessings cited in this book:

1. A father's blessing places and calls forth specific rulership ability in his children and his children's children.
2. A father's blessing activates success, prosperity, and creativity in his children.
3. A father's blessing overrules every other blessing and every curse spoken over the seed.

These paternal blessings are characterized by four overriding qualities:

1. Futuristic longevity of purpose.
2. An overriding desire to collaborate with God's purpose.
3. A willingness to seek God's face for a vision of what the future holds for your children.
4. A commitment to purposeful, daily activities that facilitate God's fulfillment of His divine will for your children.

5
Discover Your Child's Destiny

Perhaps the greatest challenge you and I will ever face as parents is discovering God's destiny and purpose for our children and then guiding them toward its fulfillment. Difficult or not, we cannot escape our God-ordained responsibility to raise up the next generation to hear and obey His voice. The future of our children and our children's children literally depends on our obedience to God as parents of *firstborn seed.*

If we truly want to fully collaborate with God's purposes in our children's lives, then we must ask four major questions, seek their answers, and act on God's desires.

1. What is God's purpose for godly seed?
2. What is God's intention for this particular child of promise?
3. What is my role as a parent?
4. Does God still bless through a generational anointing?

God's Purpose for Godly Seed

The first clue to God's eternal purpose for our children can be found at the beginning, in the Garden of Eden where

God introduced the first man and woman to His revolutionary concepts of marriage, sex, and reproduction. If we understand God's purpose for marriage, then we can begin to understand His purpose for the children that are produced in a healthy marriage.

God told Adam and Eve in Genesis 1:28 that they were to be fruitful, to multiply, and to replenish the earth and rule over it. He expects us to be willing to bring forth seed. Adam and Eve were only the first of many *generational links* in the long-range plan of God.

Children are not merely a fruit of marriage. They are not merely an afterthought that comes as a consequence of the fulfillment of our need for sexual intimacy.

It is the call of the next generation within our loins that impels us to engage in sexual intercourse. Yes, there is a place for sexual intimacy in marriage for purposes of union, closeness, and pleasure, but there is a greater and more urgent need within our spirits to regenerate ourselves in the generations to come.

The life of each eternal spirit is rooted and fulfilled in the eternal God. This life calls for longevity to fulfill the Creator's eternal purposes. This holy call energizes itself in us as a sexual urge. It is the eternal nature of our spirits that races into the future, pursuing life through succeeding generations!

Sexual intercourse may then be described as "the mutual fulfillment of two spirits made one by covenant love, that seeks to *externalize* the fruit of that union." New life is therefore begotten out of a covenant love relationship. This spirit of love shares the very nature of God, and it actualizes itself in and through the life of a newborn child.

God's eternal nature pervades everything He says and does among us. His investment in His created children and

His need for the partnership of man in this propagation of seed all reflect His eternal mode of existence and thought, manifested in our *temporary* existence. His eternal purpose for marriage is to produce godly seed who will fulfill His purposes in the generations to come.

Contrasted with the eternal purposes of God are the shortsighted perceptions and purposes of members of the "liberated generation." These "enlightened" ones like to press their case for "freedom" using the pseudo-power created in the emotions of a lost generation with catchphrases such as "women's rights," "choice rights," "contraceptive devices," and "abortion rights." The fact is that they are mistaken. They have no authority to change God's original intent at creation, nor can they alter His purposeful creation of our physical bodies for the regeneration of promised seed.

The avowed "right" of a woman to have or not to have a child is totally buried and rendered irrelevant in the presence of the prior, ultimate, and divine purpose and rights of the God of creation. We may choose to plant our thrones at the edge of the sea and command the waves of the sea to retreat, but sooner or later the overwhelming and unheeding waves of the ocean will thrust aside every argument, complaint, and demand.

The secret to the seed is God and His purposes. God is the "Senior Partner" in this covenant partnership of propagating seed and replenishing the earth. It is imperative that we affirm the Father's supreme purpose, will, and authority in the conception of every child.

When we understand that God works only according to His eternal purposes, then we will simply stand in awe and participate with humility, anticipation, and excitement in the bringing forth of new seed—properly called and regarded as *God's heritage.*

Since we do not belong to ourselves, but to our Maker, we must learn what His desires are in our generation (1 Cor.

6:20). These things directly affect our thoughts and actions toward our seed, our children of promise.

Remember the Eternal Nature of God's Spoken Word

God's eternal nature pervades all created things. It also pervades His unchanging Word, which flowed directly from the heart and mind of God. God's Word reflects the eternal nature of its divine Source, and it unites with the Spirit of God to regenerate itself as a living Word in the hearts of generation after generation.

When God speaks a word, its intended mission gives it purpose, provides its life, ensures its longevity, and propels it into the future toward its intended end.

Just as a spoken word requires a listening ear to transfer its message to another heart and mind, so the eternal purposes of God require an attentive heart, willing to deposit its riches in another generation. The eternal Father is always breathing out divine purpose and intentions from His inexhaustible Spirit. He is always seeking ready and receptive incubators for His living Word. The eternal Word of God specifically seeks the spirit (womb) of a woman and the spirit (heart) of a man, who are willing to collaborate and perform God's eternal purposes in their generation.

God's Word is filled with prophetic intention. It is pregnant with life because it contains the hope of God for the restoration of His created world. The arrowhead of that sent Word is God's plan for the salvation and restoration of the world of nations.

God's Purpose Is to Restore All Things

An eternal drama unfolds in the first and second chapters of the book of Genesis. God, the perfect Creator, created a perfect world out of His love and divine purpose. The world had the perfection of form, light, order, and harmony. It bore the marks of God's perfection and He was pleased with His creation—a created masterpiece ordained to be the recipient and receptacle of His love!

The Purpose of Seed

After the fall of man in the Garden, God made a second great move, one marked by His spoken prophecy to Eve and her eternal adversary, Satan. Before the foundations of the earth, God had already provided a way to restore fallen man and destroy the works of the enemy!

God simultaneously pronounced death to the evil one and life to the seed of the woman. It was a promise for the future, but, once spoken by God, the word took on all of its properties of life, restoration, and redemption.

In Genesis 3:15, God told the fallen angel called Satan, *"And I will put enmity between thee and the woman, and between thy seed and her seed; it shall bruise thy head, and thou shalt bruise his heel."* Once uttered by the Creator, this prophetic word became a living, dynamic, purpose-filled resolution and intention of God.

This word of purpose and promise expresses God's divine desire for the restoration of the generations of man.

God's desire is invested in the receiver of His eternal purposes and treasures. His plan is in the seed of the woman!

God, in "senior partnership," now seeks the cooperation of the man or woman. He places eternal treasures and responsibilities in the frail hands of His creatures. God intends to see His Word become "flesh" in generation after generation, following the lead of His only begotten Son. Thus the purpose and potential of bringing God's transforming life to the world for each generation is planted in the life of every seed of a woman.

The drama is always the same, whether the players are the seed of women before the birth of Christ, Christ Himself, or the seed of blood-washed women of God today who are destined to proclaim the light of Christ to yet unborn generations. The seed of woman, the sons and daughters of men, are called and ordained to crush the head of the enemy. Meanwhile, the great deceiver has made every effort to be the great "seed-stealer."

Prerequisites for Bearing and Raising Seed

If we are to completely fulfill our Maker's divine intention and properly rear and guide our seed into their destinies, then we need to meet several prerequisites.

1. *We must be aware of the needs of the people.* We need to be totally aware of the world into which our seed must be sown. God plants His seed in us to restore the world—our generation and the generation to come—back to Himself. What is the state of that environment? Is there lawlessness, disorder, and perversity? Is the nation of your seed suffering under large-scale, burdensome oppression from Satan? Does your nation desperately need a deliverer? Ask yourself, "Does my nation need a godly man or women to disciple it?"

   It is our *awareness of the needs of our people* that provides fertility to our bodies as divine seed-bearers. We are moved beyond ourselves when we, like our Lord, feel the oppression of a nation and perceive the reared head of Satan, the oppressor.

   Understanding God's divine intention for the seed of woman to crush the head of the oppressor, the godly woman makes the vital connection. She says, as Mary did thousands of years before, *"Be it* [done] *unto me according to thy word"* (Luke 1:38). Like Rachel of old, she prays, *"Give me children, or else I die"* (Gen. 30:1). Like the barren woman who births a prophet to her nation, she prays, *"Give unto thine handmaid a man child, then I will give him unto the LORD"* (1 Sam. 1:11). She now echoes the Hebrew midwives of Moses' day, "I will save this one." (See Exodus 15–21.) Men and women of God, moved by divine compassion, now say like Adam and Eve, *"God... hath appointed me another seed"* (Gen. 4:25).

The Word reveals that Samuel, Moses, Joseph, David, Jesus, and many others were all conceived and born into a world in which evil predominated.

a. In *Samuel's* day, the priests committed abominable deeds even at the door of the temple. God said, *"And I will raise me up a faithful priest"* (1 Sam. 2:35). Hannah was the seed-bearer who unknowingly responded to God.

b. *Moses* rose to prominence in Pharaoh's house, stumbled as a self-made deliverer, and yet managed to answer God's call for a God-sent deliverer when the children of Israel were afflicted with hard bondage. *"And God heard their groanings....Now Moses kept the flock"* (Exod. 2:24; 3:1).

c. *Othniel* entered the world and answered God's call. *"And when the children of Israel cried unto the LORD, the LORD raised up a deliverer to the children of Israel, who delivered them, even Othniel the son of Kenaz, Caleb's younger brother"* (Judg. 3:9).

d. *John the Baptist* was born and sent to turn the hearts of the fathers to the children in a world typified by disobedience and the affliction of children (Luke 1:17). His generation deserved only the curse of God, but, instead, God sent John to proclaim the coming Messiah.

2. *We must always remember the purpose of God for the seed.* The principle of reproduction was ordained to produce

seeds of promise and purpose. Jesus has finished the great work of salvation, but God continues to deliver new generations in the world by the redeemed seed of woman, who continue to crush Satan's head in their generation.

This principle of reproduction must be appropriated in every generation. Sarah, the wife of Abraham, appropriated this principle and brought forth the seed of promise through which the Savior of the world redeemed our fallen race. She was a vital *generational link* in the fulfillment of God's purpose.

The principle of equivalent effect, revealed in Genesis 3:15:

a. Empowered Ruth to seek seed of Boaz (Ruth 4:12).

b. Activated Rachel to earnestly desire seed (Gen. 30:1, 22).

c. Stirred the harlot Rahab to righteous action (Josh. 2).

d. Forgave the sin of David and produced Solomon from the seed of Bathsheba (2 Sam. 12:24).

When a *seed-giver* (a man) and a *seed-bearer* (a woman) know and submit to the purposes of God, then they will experience an ongoing and dynamic life-giving relationship with God. This yielding of heart and spirit produces the creative possibility of engendering seed that will become pregnant with purpose.

In one sense, God is always speaking and sowing His seed by the Holy Spirit. But God has sovereignly chosen us as partners in His divine enterprise. By His choice, His seed looks for a fertile place in which to lodge itself, and thus to become flesh for the fulfillment of its divine purpose.

3. *We must earnestly desire seed of purpose.* The seed-receiver and bearer (the woman) must earnestly desire seeds of purpose. She must appropriate God's purpose for herself and her seed. *"Be it unto* ***me*** *according to thy word"* (Luke

1:38, emphasis added). This is the response of faith that releases God's covenantal word and births deliverers for nations, generations, and eternity.

Once parents accept the call and responsibility to have a child of purpose and declare their intention to God in the face of the enemy, God again begins to enact His plan of the ages in and through the life of that seed. God's spoken word is activated in the spirit world and His original intention again is fulfilled.

This miraculous process requires men and women who recognize God's call, affirm His purpose, and covenant with Him to offer their child of promise back to God *to become part of the generational and ongoing work of God in the salvation of the world.*

4. *We must be aware of the devices of the seed-devourer.* The seed-bearer receiver must learn to recognize and counteract the devices of the seed-devourer, whose sole intention and work is to steal, kill, and destroy seeds of promise. God's declaration in Genesis 3:15 not only foretold that the woman's seed would crush Satan's head, it also established an irreconcilable enmity between the two. That means determined warfare is established between parents or caregivers and the destructive evil designs planned against our children.

   Since that fateful confrontation, Satan's every effort has been aimed at destroying or delaying God's purpose by destroying the life or effectiveness of the woman's seed. Prenatal, perinatal, and postnatal attacks on a woman's seed predominate and abound in our generation, as they did in nearly every generation before us. Many great deliverers and leaders in the Bible and in church history have had to overcome attacks by the enemy from the time of their conception to the end of their days. This makes it absolutely imperative that the seed-giver and the seed-bearer join in agreement with the God of the seed to preserve life.

God's Purpose and Intention for Your Child of Promise

Godly parents need to discover God's particular call for their children if they are to effectively help guide them through childhood to maturity. Mary and Joseph heard the prophetic word of the angel concerning their unique Son of promise. They evidently trained Jesus to fulfill God's Word spoken of Him because they knew His destiny.

As parents of God's seed, do we have to labor and struggle to discover God's intention for each of our children? Is there a general word or work that God has for each consecrated child? There are several facets to the answers for these questions. The first step is to *see how God operates.*

God's *modus operandi* (method of operation) remains unchanging and unchanged. We can therefore see clear patterns and purposes in His relationships with those who have gone before us. We need to learn these patterns so we can more effectively work *with* Him to fulfill His purposes in our lives and in the lives of our children.

The Divine Pattern for the Selection of Godly Leaders

These patterns stand out in God's Word and in human experience with Him because they appear again and again in the history of God's work in the earth:

1. *God creates and calls forth seed equipped with particular abilities and strengths to fulfill His plan for a particular people, nation, or generation.* God matches our children's strengths with a nation's current and particular needs. Our seed may be destined to become national deliverers, prophets, leaders, or servants of the people, as was the case with Moses, Isaiah, and Joshua. In every case, God has a sovereign

plan for our seed that is in-line with His eternal purposes. That plan is determined by the needs of the people at that time.

2. *God works generationally.* Many times, God calls forth an entire line or family of prophets, priests, kings, or healers. For example, God designated David's family as a royal family from which would come kings and queens from generation to generation. He set apart Aaron and his sons as priests who would serve Him forever (1 Chron. 23:13). God set apart the entire tribe of Levi and ordained them as a tribe of priests or ministers in His house from generation to generation (Num. 18:1–2).

3. *God often calls forth an individual who is an unknown out of a nation or from an unknown family to perform a major task for that nation.* God personally and sovereignly chooses His servants even before their births. These seeds of divine potential are equipped with all the necessary requirements for receiving the call. This is a perfect description of David, the shepherd boy from a remote area and unknown family of a threatened nation. By God's design, he was to form the most powerful nation of his day, serve as a type and shadow as well as a precursor of God's Messiah, and establish standards of worship and intimacy with God that few, if any of us, can match today.

4. *God delights in choosing the base things and the humble things to accomplish His purposes in the earth* (1 Cor. 1:26–29). God looks for men and women who simply fear, obey, and love Him. He regards *"the low estate of his handmaiden,"* as Mary said (Luke 1:48). *"And his mercy is on them* ***that fear him*** *from generation to generation"* (verse 50, emphasis added). *"He hath...exalted them* ***of low degree****"* (verse 52, emphasis added). God seems to delight in choosing for leadership humble persons who better understand authority and obedience to law and who are less inclined to prideful

domination when they become exalted to positions of prominence and influence.

Hilkiah was a simple priest from the little tribe of Benjamin, living in Anathoth. We hear nothing more of him after his son was born, but that son was a child of destiny. Hilkiah may be forgotten by many, but he will always be honored by God as the simple priest who raised up his seed in the fear of the Lord in a nation filled with apostasy and sin. That seed of promise was Jeremiah, one of the greatest prophets who ever lived.

5. *God sovereignly gives gifts and abilities to individuals and then anoints, appoints, and sends them forth to perform particular tasks and roles.* It is His sovereign right to empower a child with talents, gifts, and abilities. Being God, He creates our seed according to His higher purposes and then matches their gifts with the needs of His selected field of service for their lives. Even in the local church, the Holy Spirit gives supernatural gifts to our children, *"dividing to every man severally as he will"* (1 Cor. 12:11).

What Is My Role as a Parent?

As parents, are we simply supposed to receive God's grace and raise our children blindly, or are we partners and co-laborers with God in the salvation of the world? To what extent does God use the authority given to man to call forth leadership gifts in His sons? To what extent does God add His favor and blessing to the desires of parents for their children's purpose?

Many times, God has worked closely with the parents of great leaders in the past. In fact, many times men and women have actively intervened on behalf of their seed and for the purpose of the fulfillment of God's prophetic intention for their seed.

1. *Moses would never have lived to deliver Israel if his mother had not intervened to save his life.* Despite Pharaoh's strict

order to kill all newborn Hebrew males, Moses' mother *"saw him that he was a goodly child,* [so] *she hid him three months"* (Exod. 2:2). Moses came from the tribe of Levi, and it was not unexpected that a national leader should arise out of a priestly tribe. However, that mother actively strategized to save her selected seed!

2. *Jacob blessed his children differentially.* He had a unique blessing for each child. He prophesied over Reuben, *"Thou shalt not excel"* (Gen. 49:4). Jacob told Judah, *"Thy brethren shall praise* [you]*...thy father's children shall bow down before thee"* (verse 8). He told Joseph, *"The blessings of thy father have prevailed above the blessings of my progenitors unto the utmost bound of the everlasting hills"* (verse 26). This is a classic example of a father commanding the blessings of God and speaking them into the lives of his children to override circumstances and adversity. God not only honored this father's spoken blessing and vocational call for his seed, but He also honored his blessing *"unto the utmost bound of the everlasting hills"*!

3. *God searches for men and women of vision who will boldly call forth the God-given strengths in their seed and match them with the identified needs of their nation.* He raises up parents and leaders who will dare to speak forth the history of their nation and predetermine the course of that history as they bless God's seed. Time and again, God gave parents like Abraham, Isaac, Jacob, Mary and Joseph, David and Bathsheba, and Aaron clear visions of the part their children would play in their nation's destiny. This typifies the heart of the Father God as He Himself watches over the history of men and nations.

4. *Bathsheba stategized for her son Solomon to become king and heir of David.* David's lineage carried the seed of promise, and Jesus was to be called both the Root and the Offspring of David (Rev. 22:16). The book of 1 Kings recounts the

deliberate actions of Bathsheba, the mother of Solomon, who countered the political maneuvering of another son by a different woman.

The king had already promised the throne to Solomon, but Adonijah was playing a dangerous game to steal the throne from Solomon as soon as David died.

Bathsheba moved quickly upon the advice of the prophet Nathan. She presumptuously sought an audience with the king and reminded him of his promise to appoint her son Solomon as king. She won his support and the throne for Solomon!

Was this the strategy of an ambitious, position-seeking mother, or was it the preservation of her son's calling of God to a position of divine, predestined purpose? I believe it was both! God honored Bathsheba! But God also had a predetermined plan for this son of His. Solomon was destined to be a significant link in the generational chain and genealogical lineage of the Messiah.

5. *Did the anguished cry of a childless barren woman precipitate the birth and call of Samuel, the greatest priest and judge of Israel?* Did Hannah's desperate promise to God to return her seed to Him change the destiny of her nation, or was her cry perfectly timed with the purposes of God for her nation? The fact is that God had to find a faithful priest because the priestly line of Eli was to be cut off. God had also found in Hannah a woman who longed for a child and who would keep her promise to return her seed to the Lord. Did the miracle begin with the barren womb and its cry for a child? I believe it did!

   God still looks for women with *"a sorrowful spirit"* (1 Sam. 1:15) who anticipate the gift of children and who can see the possibilities for the victory of God through their children's lives. This is reflected in the anointed song of Hannah (1 Sam. 2:1–10).

6. *The quick action* of *the earthly parents of Jesus, the holy Child with the messianic call, is perhaps the greatest example of parents who intervened under God's guidance to preserve His Seed.* What was the role of Joseph and Mary in saving and preserving the Savior of the world? Joseph believed God and agreed to "*take away* [the] *reproach*" (Luke 1:25) of the pregnant girl he was engaged to. He later gathered his wife and the Seed of promise at a moment's notice to flee to Egypt to preserve the Lord's life from a vengeful ruler in Israel.

   Mary, His mother, must have often said, "I must tell Jesus again of His 'Father's business.' I must give Him the care and food He needs to grow in stature before God, His Father. I must take Him to the synagogue to listen to the rabbis. I must always ponder in my heart the promise for this Child: *'Thou shalt call his name JESUS: for he shall save his people from their sins'* (Matt. 1:21)." She not only preserved her seed, but she also preserved the purpose for her seed!

What Can We Learn from God's Modus Operandi?

How are we to know God's prophetic intention for each child? There are several precedents in the Scriptures that help us discover God's purpose for our seed:

1. God will sovereignly determine and design His will for each child. He reveals His will through multiple sources, including parental revelation and spoken prophecies or words brought by an apostle, prophet, evangelist, pastor, or teacher, or even by the child himself.
2. The gifts and talents of your children will precipitate God's call on their lives and their selection for certain tasks. Your child will know when those emerging gifts reveal themselves, and God will give your child the desire and the sure knowledge of God's call. Parents are to lovingly watch over their children's revealed or stated purpose and to prayerfully train each of them.

3. God will honor your desires for your children when they line up with God's purposes for the nations and the glory of His name. Selfish ambitions or desires on the part of parents to fulfill their own goals through their children will result in pain and possible failure in their children's lives. We must pursue only the known and confirmed purpose of God for our children.
4. God will use *the ministry of the prophet* to confirm the word already spoken into the life of the child and the hearts of the parents. A prophetic word should not be sought without the joint participation of parents and pastor. When a child receives a prophetic word, there should be a confirming witness among the child's significant caregivers.
5. God uses the *foresight of the father,* with his insightful predictions of the future, his people, or his nation to call forth gifts and purpose in his sons and daughters. The blessing of the father is tied to the divine hope as well as to God's search for vessels of honor. Through a father's spoken word of blessing, God will cause the potential within the man's seed to be released for the performance of the already spoken Word.

   The parents of godly seed must closely collaborate with God from the conception of their seed to the fulfillment of God's purposes. Once a word of blessing is spoken by a parent, that parent must begin a lifelong process of purposeful and goal-oriented guidance and ministry to and on behalf of the child of promise. Then parents must trust God to add His increase.
6. God blesses and honors the desires of parents when they proclaim His Word on behalf of their seed. He is committed to watching over His Word to perform it (Jer. 1:12). When parents "command a blessing" with prophetic purpose on a child, their obedience reflects their joint

activity with God the Father. God will hasten to perform that word. Such an act on the part of parents empowers and activates the quick outworking of the directed and goal-oriented word.

Does God Still Bless through a Generational Anointing?

The principle of generational anointing, or blessing, finds its roots in the nature of God, who created things to reproduce after their own kind. Have you noticed that it is not unusual for families of singers to produce singers, and families of craftsmen to produce craftsmen?

The high priest's son, who was born with the predisposition to perform priestly functions in ancient Israel, probably watched his father bear the blood of atonement for the sins of the people to God once a year. It wouldn't be unusual for him to share his father's fears and joys and develop a natural desire to carry on the work of his father. That boy would surely become a priest one day.

We should add some "formal" preparation experiences to our children's natural patterns of observation and imitation. Special acts of anointing or consecration (such as the Jewish observance of the bar mitzvah service for young men entering manhood) would help embed and seal the prophetic word of God in the hearts and minds of the seed, as well as release the blessing of God.

The Lord Jesus said that He spoke the things that He had received from His Father (John 12:49). God wants us to speak good things to our children. He expects us to live godly lives before them and to model righteousness and true spirituality in our homes. This kind of consistent training and mentoring builds a rich foundation in their hearts and minds that will serve them well in the years that follow.

God still redeems new generations of fallen men through the ministry of new generations of redeemed men. It is useless for each new generation of young believers to "start all over again" in their knowledge of God and wisdom levels—especially when the generation before them has a wealth of experience, training, and wisdom to pass along to them. Even more importantly, the new generation of "Timothys" deserves to receive the same impartation and "weapon" that Timothy received from the apostle Paul and others:

> *Neglect not the gift that is in thee, which was given thee by prophecy, with the laying on of the hands of the presbytery.* (1 Tim. 4:14)

> *This charge I commit unto thee, son Timothy, according to the prophecies which went before on thee, that thou by them mightest war a good warfare.* (1 Tim. 1:18)

The Genesis 3:15 Declarations

> *And I will put enmity between thee and the woman, and between thy seed and her seed; it shall bruise thy head, and thou shalt bruise his heel.* (Gen. 3:15)

God's word of judgment to Satan in Genesis 3:15 imparted a generational word of promise to Adam and Eve that carried three major declarations:

1. God made a *generational promise* to Adam and Eve in Genesis 3:15. It was a guarantee of victory as well as a word of grace that would comfort the first parents and every generation on the earth after them. God's spoken word transmitted *generational anointing* through the seed of Adam and Eve directly to us and to the generations that will follow us.

2. God imposed a *generational responsibility* on every parent in Genesis 3:15. The promise of victory for the seed of woman would not be obtained without warfare. God charged the first parents and every parent who would follow, with *generational responsibility* for conceiving, bearing, and

rearing seed after their kind. Their seed was to bear responsibility for every generation after them.

3. God also gave our race a divine means and an inner drive or instinct for *generational preservation* in Genesis 3:15. Before the fall of Adam and Eve, man was an eternal creature—even his physical existence faced no danger of decay, disintegration, attack, or death. Once sin entered the picture, the life of God's highest creation could be snuffed out in a moment, and it would certainly end after a relatively brief lifetime on the earth.

   God's law of reproduction now took on a new and vital importance. It was man's only means to preserve his generations. It was God's way to help Adam and his descendants live with divine purpose and carry on God's eternal purposes from generation to generation through the seed.

   This intense motivation to preserve the next generation empowered Noah, Abraham, Jacob, and Joseph, the earthly father of Jesus, *"to keep seed alive upon the face of all the earth"* (Gen. 7:3).

The single greatest force in the world is a strong sense of family love and unity combined with God's anointing.

The strength of a God-anointed family fulfilling God's purposes in love and unity provides the ideal incubator and training ground for *transgenerational blessings.* The prophet Joel told the inhabitants of Israel,

> *Hear this, ye old men, and give ear, all ye inhabitants of the land. Hath this been in your days, or even in the days of your fathers? Tell ye your children of it, and let your children tell their children, and their children another generation.* (Joel 1:2–3)

Joel was speaking to a sinful generation of the judgment they had experienced, but we should be even more eager to share the good things of God with our seed. It is knowledge of the truth that will preserve the life of our children.

The preservation of the seed is the reason a father *"leaveth an inheritance to his children's children"* (Prov. 13:22). For this reason a man shall *"leave his father and his mother, and shall cleave unto his wife"* (Gen. 2:24). This is also the reason a man must preserve his family with paternal qualities of strength and covering, and a mother must shield her home with similar strong instincts for preserving, nurturing, and guarding the seed.

It is God's plan for the strong family unit to prolong its God-given life and anointing from one generation to the next. It is through the family that God preordained the salvation of the world. The Bible carefully traces the genealogical line of Jesus because this was the lifeline bearing the promise of salvation for the world. Jesus Himself declared that He was the *"root and the offspring of David"* (Rev. 22:16). By this statement, He affirmed the *role of genealogical promise.* The work of God in blessing family lines continues today, and along with it comes responsibilities and vows.

This then is the divine *modus operandi.* It is the pattern we are to follow. The Scriptures reveal God's manner of operation. Since God never changes, we may conclude that God's purpose for a family may be linked to a generational purpose for that family. The fact that all prophets do not produce prophets, and that some "preachers' kids" become rebellious atheists is no reason for God to change His way of operating. Nor should parents lose hope, strength, or purpose because some children have chosen to step out of God's purposes.

Aaron: The Generational Call

The following selected Scripture references expose the way God thinks and the way He prefers to operate. It is a divinely economical way. It's the generational way.

And take...Aaron thy brother, and his sons with him...that he may minister unto me in the priest's office. (Exod. 28:1)

I will sanctify also both Aaron and his sons, to minister to me in the priest's office. (Exod. 29:44)

And when Aaron lighteth the lamps at even, he shall burn incense upon it, a perpetual incense before the LORD *throughout your generations.* (Exod. 30:8)

So they shall wash their hands and their feet, that they die not: and it shall be a statute for ever to them, even to him and to his seed throughout their generations. (verse 21)

And Moses said unto Aaron and to his sons, Boil the flesh at the door of the tabernacle...and there eat it with the bread that is in the basket of consecrations, as I commanded, saying, Aaron and his sons shall eat it. (Lev. 8:31)

It was God's divine intention to bless and consecrate for service both a priest and his sons. This is the way God ensures longevity of purpose and the fulfilment of destiny.

God's Eternal Anointing Extends to the Generations

God carefully designed the structure, function, and interaction of the family unit. Fathers are ordained to yearn for posterity, for seed that will fulfill purpose. Mothers are formed by God not only to reproduce, but also to carefully train and instruct the seed. God has designed the family to pass on blessings, talents, and gifts from one generation to the next. These dynamic operational forces are transgenerational, and they work in line with God's plan for the inheritance of blessings.

Punishment and Curses Are Also Generational

The Bible account in the book of Leviticus of the curse of Aaron's sons is full of pathos. In spite of all the blessings and anointing upon this celebrated and set apart family of priests, Aaron's sons, Nadab and Abihu, *"offered strange fire before the LORD, which he commanded them not"* (Lev. 10:1). God's judgment was sharp and quick. Fire from the Lord literally devoured those young men of promise and anointing!

God again invested His trust in Aaron's seed when He reached out with fresh responsibilities for Eleazar and Ithamar, Aaron's two remaining sons, that same day. As He had done earlier with Nadab and Abihu, God meticulously prescribed their duties for them. But for the second time that day, the seed of Aaron veered away from God's specific ordinances for bringing the sin offering. Moses angrily rebuked Aaron's sons but softened when the father of those irresponsible sons recounted the tragedies and misfortune he and his sons had suffered that day. God, through Moses, spared the sons of promise.

The sin of Eli's sons represents one of the greatest offenses against God's holiness recorded in the Bible. Every parent should carefully consider his or her responsibility to properly correct and train the next generation in light of God's cursing of Eli's house (and of his generation).

God had instructed Eli and his sons in all functions of the priest's office. This father and his sons were part of the family line granted a perpetual priesthood, generations before, through Aaron and his sons (Exod. 29:9). The blessings and honor associated with this office were many, and the priests were adequately provided for.

However, Hophni and Phinehas, the sons of Eli, broke the law of God with complete disregard for His holiness and authority. First, they did not want the portions of cooked meat set aside from the sacrifices for the priests. They refused to wait for the meat of the sacrifices to cook long enough for the fat to be burned off. The two sons of Eli actually commanded their servant to forcefully take portions of meat for them from the unprepared flesh (1 Sam. 2:12–17).

Even worse, these priests of the Most High God dared to openly commit adultery *"with the women that assembled at the door of the tabernacle of the congregation"* (1 Sam. 2:22).

The Bible described these young priests as *"sons of Belial"* who did not know the Lord (verse 12). In fact, the public sin of these two brothers was so disgusting that the Scriptures say, *"Wherefore the sin of the young men was very great before the LORD: for men abhorred the offering of the LORD"* (1 Sam. 2:17).

The sin of the sons of Eli were so great that God had to break the generational covenant He had made with the tribe of Levi to remove reproach from His house. That line of the priesthood was cut off, and the prophet Samuel arose to restore God's clear voice to his generation. God's judgment to sinful priests is direct and deadly: *"But ye are departed out of the way; ye have caused many to stumble at the law; ye have corrupted the covenant of Levi, saith the LORD of hosts"* (Mal. 2:8). God declares to covenant-breaking priests, *"I will curse your blessings"* and *"Behold, I will corrupt your seed"* (verses 2–3).

Did Eli teach and train his sons? He probably did train them up to a point, for it was the practice of the priests to train their sons. Something was terribly wrong, however. God asked Eli, "Why do you honor your sons more than Me?" (See 1 Samuel 2:29.) For whatever reason, by the time Eli's sons were old enough to minister in the house of God, they *"hearkened not unto the voice of their father"* (1 Sam. 2:25).

God judged Eli's house because Eli had failed to restrain and control his seed: *"Behold...I will cut off thine arm, and the arm of thy father's house, that there shall not be an old man in thine house"* (verse 31). The generational blessing God had pronounced upon the generations of Levi was halted and a curse of death was placed on that family line because of the sins of Eli's sons and because Eli was unwilling to restrain them.

Even in this situation, God's eternal purpose is revealed and His method of working through the generations again surfaces. God spoke through a man of God, saying, *"And I will raise me up a faithful priest...I will build him a sure house* [generation]*; and he shall walk before mine anointed for ever"* (1 Sam 2:35).

Through the prophet Malachi, many generations after the death of Eli and his sons, God said He would provide a way to purify the sons of Levi and make them fit for priestly service again.

> *Behold, I will send my messenger, and he shall prepare the way before me: and the Lord, whom ye seek, shall suddenly come to his temple, even the messenger of the covenant...he is like a refiner's fire, and like fullers' soap: and he shall sit as a refiner and purifier of silver: and he shall purify the sons of Levi, and purge them as gold and silver, that they may offer unto the LORD an offering in righteousness.*
> (Mal. 3:1–3)

The promise continues in chapter 4 of Malachi:

> *Behold, I will send you Elijah the prophet before the coming of the great and dreadful day of the LORD: and he shall turn the heart of the fathers to the children, and the heart of the children to their fathers, lest I come and smite the earth with a curse.* (Mal. 4:5–6)

What was the weakness of Eli?

1. He honored his sons above God (1 Sam. 2:29).
2. He knew his sons were breaking God's law, but *"he restrained them not"* (1 Sam. 3:13).

What was the curse Eli received for his sin?

His sons, and his opportunity for generations of sons after him, were cut off.

This example of defiant and disobedient sons being cursed with death may be seen as a blessing in disguise. God, as well as any truly godly parent, would not stand by and watch repeated generational sin and offense negatively affect repeated generations. It appears that God at times permits no recurring multi-generational sin. He incisively cuts off the influence until a new and fresh child is born who can receive the intended blessing and faithfully perform the priestly, kingly, or prophetic office.

What was God's promise?

God promised to send a second Elijah (John the Baptist) and the "messenger of the covenant" (Jesus Christ).

The strategy would be to raise up leaders who would teach the fathers of families, reveal the judgment of God for disobedience, and build up parents who would train the next generation of children of destiny.

1. To "*turn the heart of the fathers to the children*" (Mal. 4:6). This new generation of fathers would train their children well, restrain them from evil, and honor the law of God more than they feared their children. These fathers would have an increased regard for their children and for the welfare of their children. They would focus less on themselves and more on ensuring that their children are not abused and neglected.
2. To turn "*the disobedient to the wisdom of the just*" (Luke 1:17). God intended to train, correct, reprove, and disciple the children, or the rebellious generations, to be obedient to God's law. Knowledge of God's law, and obedience to it, is wisdom. God was determined to restore the generational,

covenantal promise He made to Levi. It is the role of godly adults in every generation to assume the position of teachers of wisdom. A child repeatedly chooses to do wrong when he is not taught love for God and loving obedience to His law. This is the wisdom of the just!

3. To refine, purify, and purge the fallen generations so that they once again may serve Him in righteousness (Mal. 3:3).

First, God chose Aaron and his sons to be a perpetual priesthood before Him. Then God chose the tribe of Levi and his generations after him. Now God has a chosen generation, a royal priesthood—He has our sons and daughters! And they will inherit not curses but blessings! And the curse will be effectively removed.

What does God seek?

1. God seeks *godly seed* (Mal. 2:15).
2. God seeks *seeds of promise* who will inherit blessings and priestly responsibility.
3. God seeks *children for office* in His kingdom and in the nations of the world. He sovereignly selects and equips our seed for these positions.
4. God seeks *parental collaborators* with whom He can work in training their children for office.
5. God seeks to *give prophetic direction and confirmation* to godly parents to help them direct their seed forward to the completion of God's purpose in their lives.
6. God seeks *parents who want to raise up godly seed after their own kind.* God literally wants us to reproduce ourselves. When a godly family has a strong transgenerational gift, that gift is to be passed on from parents to children and from children to grandchildren. We are to celebrate and declare that gift. God will honor our actions.

7. God seeks *parents who will properly observe and train their children.* We must train them and restrain them while activating their talents. This will happen naturally as we cooperate with God.
8. God seeks *households where every activity and function is centered around the preparation of the seed of promise.*
9. God seeks fathers and mothers who will *"command" a purposeful and directional blessing* on their children.

God has made it clear that He wants communities of families dedicated to raising seed of destiny. They are to be the salt of the earth, the preservers, the movers and the shapers of their generation.

Discovering your child's destiny and committing yourself to shape that child's life in accordance with the known divine purpose is the key to ensuring God's will for His kingdom establishment.

Now that you have read this chapter, stop and complete this checklist. It may help you fulfill your calling as a mentor and nurturer of the next generation.

Parents' Checklist

How to Discover God's Specific Intention for Your Child

Mark "Yes" or "No" after reading each statement.

Yes/No **Role/Activity of the Parent**

1. Like the mother of Moses, I perceive that my child is a "proper" child.
2. I bless my children (to bless means to release potential).
3. I bless my children differentially because I understand that each child has a different call.

Yes/No **Role/Activity of the Parent**

4. I bless my children prophetically because I know it is God's will to use me to do this (just as Jacob blessed his children).

5. I bless my children futuristically because I realize that prophecies demand time to be fulfilled.

6. I bless my children based on my vision because prophecies demand a parent's vision.

7. I am a man or woman of vision, with a sense of *destiny* and of *history* (the future and the past).

8. I watch carefully and observe my children's gifts, abilities, strengths, and weaknesses.

9. I know that I can do this because it is part of my natural gifting that comes from God with parenthood.

10. I am aware of what God is telling me about His prophetic intention for my children. I can speak into my children's life, and God will honor that pure word.

11. I am aware of, I write down, and I remember every prophetic word spoken for my child. I receive the confirmed word, ponder it continually, and rehearse it before my seed.

12. I listen carefully to my children's expressed desires and to any word my children have personally received from God.

13. I dare not be afraid to reach out to God or to hear a prophetic word for my children.

14. Like Hannah, I cry out in anguish of soul for my seed.

15. I "work" the prophetic word, just as Mary and Joseph did for Jesus. I actively prepare my children to fulfill God's exact and specific *spoken will* for them.

Yes/No **Role/Activity of the Parent**

16. I strategize for the destiny of my seed, like Bathsheba did for Solomon (1 Kings 1). I remember God's promise and act upon it, as Jesus did.

17. I act upon the Word. I design teaching, training, and instructional experiences for my children.

18. I maintain an ongoing collaborative relationship with God, knowing He will carefully watch over His Word to perform it.

19. I conduct goal-directed child rearing.

20. I am aware of transgenerational influences, blessings, anointings, and responsibilities.

21. I am aware of the role of the family in passing on generational gifts, teaching, and skill development.

22. I am aware that God still operates with transgenerational purpose (as He did with the families of Aaron and Levi).

23. I teach the seed of promise.

24. I tell the seed of promise of God's intention for him or her.

25. Unlike Eli, whose seed profaned God's house, I restrain my seed from breaking God's law.

26. I do not honor my children above God as Eli did.

27. I am not too timid to receive God's Word for my children.

28. I am willing to do whatever God says so that His prophetic intention will be fulfilled in my children, just as the mother of Samson would drink no strong drink (Lev. 10:9).

30. I defer my own personal wishes, desires, and agendas to what God wants for my children.

Yes/No **Role/Activity of the Parent**

31. I am willing for my seed to accept God's call.

32. I give my seed back to God the Father as Hannah, the mother of Samuel, did.

33. I ask myself, What would I prophesy of my children

...if I had all the resources?

...if I had unlimited creative ability?

...if I knew that I could not fail?

Remember: God says that you and your children have everything you need for a godly life, and you cannot fail (2 Pet. 1:3)!

6
Raising Children of Destiny

The Principle of Generational Leadership

The following is the principle of generational leadership, which has been clearly outlined in Scripture, and which has been extrapolated from a study of nature, a perusal of genetic roots of reproduction, and a look at examples of family inheritance, transmission, succession, and inheritance.

The nature of eternity demands that finite man operates intergenerationally and with a multi-generational attitude. The nature of all things created demands that life continues. That continuity is guaranteed by the principle of the seed.

The truth of eternality also demands that things be reformed, reborn, and restored to former and/or future vitality, purpose, and image. For this to take place, there must be an absolute standard for truth, a hallmark for integrity, and a divine understanding of the concept of wholeness.

Man has been created superior, has been given dominion authority, and has been given the mandate for stewardship of the earth. That domain includes the land, the resources, the systems, and the leadership of men. Man has, in effect, been endowed with a spirit of leadership that seeks the eternal welfare and good for the earth. He has also been gifted with the awesome responsibility of reproducing himself. This is the prize, the *raison d'etre* of man:

1. First, he must become a man of destiny and truth, with the ability to love justice, to be merciful, and to be willing to be a wise and godly leader.
2. Second, he must be prepared to raise up children of destiny, who will both follow and outstrip him in the pursuit of leadership of nations. The following is the divine example. It is the Father's master plan for His Son—the supreme Seed of Destiny. The pattern offers to us a *modus operandi* as we follow in His footsteps and proclaim the birth, growth, and purpose of our own seed of promise and purpose.

> *And there shall come forth a rod out of the stem of Jesse, and a Branch shall grow out of his roots: and the spirit of the LORD shall rest upon him, the spirit of wisdom and understanding, the spirit of counsel and might, the spirit of knowledge and of the fear of the LORD...he shall not judge after the sight of his eyes, neither reprove after the hearing of his ears: but with righteousness shall he judge... and reprove....The wolf also shall dwell with the lamb...* ***and a little child shall lead them****.*
>
> (Isa. 11:1–4, 6, emphasis added)

Jesus Christ, the Son of God, is the supreme model for our children of destiny. He is the First Seed of God, and all of the sons and daughters of God are predestined *"to be conformed to the image of his Son, that he might be the firstborn among many brethren"* (Rom. 8:29). From chapter 11 of the book of Isaiah, we can see that:

1. Just as young David came out of his father Jesse and ruled the nation, so would Jesus, the Son of David, sprout forth as a Branch to rule the world. This is the principle of generational leadership in

operation. God causes leaders to spring forth from the old to the new, and from the parent to the child (Isa. 11:1).

2. Jesus was anointed with the Spirit of the Lord and with the Spirit of wisdom, understanding, counsel, might, knowledge, and fear of the Lord. This supreme act of God supernaturally equipped Jesus to fulfill His purpose (Isa. 11:2).
3. Jesus did not judge *"after the sight of his eyes, neither reprove after the hearing of his ears"* (Isa. 11:3). He was not led or limited by His senses and environment; He was led by the Spirit. His counsel superseded any earthly source of counsel. He was a son of parents, but His knowledge surpassed that of His parents. He was a son of the law, but His knowledge surpassed that of His teachers. Jesus not only benefited from His earthly environment (including the instruction of His teachers), but He also abounded in the heavenly and extraordinary wisdom that came with His purpose.
4. Isaiah reveals the irony of the almighty God anointing a child to restore His kingdom and glory among men. This little child was destined to change our world forever because it was His divine destiny. Isaiah knew even then that *"a little child shall lead them"* (Isa. 11:6). Every parent of godly seed must ask, "What does this mean? Am I prepared to allow my children to lead?" It would be a child of destiny, imbued with the hopes and prayers of his parents and with the clarity and simplicity of youth, who would lead us.

The Child: The Leader

Why Did God Say, "A Little Child"?

Each child must strive in his or her struggle for survival. The only way to lead a nation in the generation to come is to raise up leaders who know how to lead. Our children must struggle and lead for their own survival.

God has ordained that a nation's survival depends on the ability of its young to survive. Struggle and leadership ensure that survival is obtained. Medical professionals tell us that the usual colds, sniffles, and routine childhood infections are actually necessary to ensure a healthy immune system with the necessary antibodies in adult life! The epistle of James says that testings and trials produce patience, and that we need to *"let patience have her perfect work, that* [we] *may be perfect and entire, wanting nothing"* (James 1:4).

The needs of our children demand that we act. Their needs can propel us into the action that is needed for our own generation to survive. Many parents may lose interest in themselves, but their abiding interest in their children's needs energizes them to purposeful, goal-directed action.

Isaiah's prophecy is steeped in a prophetic dimension. By the Spirit, he prophesied that a day would come when the children would have wisdom beyond that of their parents. Their wisdom will surpass that of their teachers. God will give them all the strengths they need for leadership. In this way, God ensures that His kingdom will continue to be established transgenerationally,

Children walk with a certain degree of purity in their perceptions. Once they perceive the will and wishes of their Master, they have no hesitation or doubt. When they hear the word, *"This is the way, walk ye in it"* (Isa. 30:21), they walk forth in confidence, unhindered by "adult" perceptions that may cause their parents to stumble.

Have you ever noticed the confidence of a young child? Although an adult may doubt his own perception of reality, a child never doubts. An adult's mind may become cluttered with memories of past failures and mistakes, and these cause him to hesitate in self-doubt. An adult's faith can become dependent on past memories, but a child moves freely ahead, unhindered and unspoiled. He looks straight ahead and moves with purpose and freedom. This proves that purity of spirit is more important than knowledge or experience. Chronological age acquisition is not as closely connected with leadership ability as we think.

According to Isaiah the prophet, there will come a day when a little child will lead. A son will lead a father. The "new generation" will lead the "old generation." This creates an age-old problem that is two-sided. Leaders from the older generation hold on to the power of leadership long after they have lost their leadership effectiveness. As a result, the young have been methodically "kept in their place" and are not perceived as leaders. When they do rise to a position of leadership, they have great difficulty getting recognition for their leadership and giftings. The apostle Paul had to address this in his epistle to young Timothy, who was pastoring a church founded by Paul: *"Let no man despise thy youth; but be thou an example"* (1 Tim. 4:12).

Why Should We Train Our Children for Leadership?

"And a little child shall lead them" (Isa. 11:6). The issue is not whether this prophecy has been fulfilled or when it will be fulfilled. There is no issue: A little child will lead, whether now or later. In a day of peace, when the Rod of Jesse rules, when the knowledge of the glory of the Lord covers the earth, then the picture will be complete. The little child will lead.

Isaiah implies that the child will be the focal point, giving direction to all that is and all that will happen in the world. It is for *the children's sake* that action will be initiated. It is *through the children* that major links will be formed. It is *because of the children* that significant decisions will be made.

I believe that the plight of the children will continue to be at the center of much of the world's battle between good and evil. Ultimately, *every nation will be judged by its treatment of its children.* Every father will be measured by the well-being of his children. A mother's level of optimism will be determined by the glory reflected in her children's children.

If the birth of a child means the extension of the race, then the life of a child means the future life of the race. Furthermore, the wealth or poverty of that child determines the state of the race.

There is, inherent in the child, the accumulated wisdom and hope of previous generations as well as the addition of new truth. If the purpose of the older generation is to teach the young, then the young will certainly gain all that the older generation has to teach, as well as the accumulated experience of their forefathers. Additionally, the young have all of the present and the untapped possibilities of the future to extend into previously unattained positions of knowledge, understanding, and wisdom. For this reason it is true to say, *"A little child shall lead them."*

Leadership depends not so much on history as upon forward movement into the future. It requires a measure of reckless abandon to tackle untried opportunities, to ride on consecutive leaps of faith—as only our children can do.

I recently asked my youngest son why he drove so quickly in the busy traffic. He answered, "Mum. I see quicker. I move quicker. And I am quicker!" He has implicit and well-founded faith in his visual sense of judgment, in himself, and in my speedy car. I relaxed and let him drive. I was confident because he was free of my apprehensions and useless suppositions from the past. He was free to be confident, to assess situations quickly for himself, and to drive me—yes, to lead me!

Many parents spend a great deal of time methodically training their children to fear what they (the parents) are afraid of. These parents diligently teach their seed to limit themselves within the narrow boundaries of inhibition that the parents have learned to live with. How many times do we recount our silly mistakes of the past (moved more by our own fears and guilt) and actually believe that we are teaching our children lessons of experience?

A child leads his parents by propelling them toward the future and forcing them away from the past. This stirs the parents into mobility and action to provide for their child's future needs. They know they must keep up with the times and actively change the future so their children's children will be provided for. What an exciting truth! As we teach youth, we actively discard our old misconceptions and become recipients of new and enriching truth and glory ourselves!

A Little Child Shall Lead Them

And a little child shall lead them!

A child not beset by needless fears.

A child uninhibited by nature's petty laws.

A child with eyes for the future only.

A child walking fully in the light of the Father's presence,

And yielding himself so fully to the law of dominion which his very presence brings to his surroundings.

So much is he like His Father God that

He pushes back the curse of fear, and gives no place to the evil one:

—no reminders of lost hope or of lost opportunities, or of lost dominion.

A little child shall lead them…

He will fully and joyfully drink of all the wealth of glory.

And as he does, more glory will spring up and he shall have no sense of waste or loss.

As he gladly partakes of the glory and gladly shares his Master's presence,

Without struggle and without fear

Without greed and without duress...

A little child enjoys his work...or is it play?

He does not need to hoard for tomorrow

For tomorrow becomes today and new glory springs up on every hand.

And what is truth if not the simple acceptance of each task, the quiet contemplation of each thing of beauty,

The peaceful fullness of all that speaks so loudly, but so clearly, of the Father's self, a willingness to do all that the Father says and a quiet endless probing of the Father's Spirit?

And with this truth, this peace, this dominion, this endless communion, and this presence of the Father's glory,

A little child shall lead us!

He shall lead us with an eternal sense of destiny, with a willingness to do all for which he has been destined—with dominion regained, with purpose fulfilled and destiny achieved.

Raising Leaders: The Example of Jesus

The lives and experiences of Joseph and Mary as they raised the Son of God and helped prepare Him for His destiny offer us a wealth of wisdom we can use in our own homes. I believe the earthly parents of Jesus Christ asked themselves a number of questions that you and I should also consider. Ask yourself these questions and ponder the answers. They speak loudly about whether we are prepared to raise up children of promise.

1. In the first place, do I wish to bear a child?
2. "Savior of the world"...a "child of destiny"...much discipleship and teaching will be required of me. Am I willing and able to do this?

3. "Savior of the world"...for service to the world...am I prepared to raise a child and then to give him up? After all, this is my child!
4. "Son of God"...am I prepared to share the fatherhood of my child with God?
5. This child, my beloved firstborn...must he really give his life for this ungodly generation?
6. We're such humble folk...would God use us to bring forth His seed?
7. He's such a strange child, intent only on doing "His Father's business" (Luke 2:49), can I bear the pain of loneliness and separation from him?
8. Did I really hear that angel? What about the words of cousin Elisabeth and of Anna? Was it all a dream? Did I really hear a sure word of prophecy?

Mary and Joseph settled questions like these and obeyed God. Mary simply answered, *"Be it unto me according to thy word"* (Luke 1:38). That "Yes!" set in motion and energized the train of events that led to the life, death, and resurrection of Jesus and the fulfillment of His purpose.

Tracing the Path of Mary and Joseph

There are several lessons that can be learned from Mary and Joseph and from the perfect life and example of Jesus Christ, God's Son of promise and purpose. Are you willing to follow in their footsteps so that your godly seed can rise up and deliver his nation?

1. See yourself as a generational link.

   The Magnificat, the spontaneous song Mary sang as she greeted Elisabeth, unmistakably places Mary and Joseph as the generational link between the past and the future.

   And his mercy is on them that fear him from generation to generation. (Luke 1:50)

He hath [helped] *his servant Israel, in remembrance of his mercy.* (Luke 1:54)

As he spake to our fathers, to Abraham, and to his seed for ever. (verse 55)

When I think of Mary as she recalled the prophetic words given by God to Abraham of old, I can almost hear her say, "I am going to bring that prophecy into being through my obedience and willingness." Mary saw herself as a generational link in the long-range plan of God.

2. *Ponder in your heart every prophetic word for your seed.*

   "But Mary kept all these things, and pondered them in her heart" (Luke 2:19). Mary had heard the prophetic word for her Son's life with her own ears, but now at His birth, the shepherds had come with a concurring prophetic word. "The angels told us, *'For unto you is born this day in the city of David a Saviour, which is Christ the Lord '* (verse 11)." What was the response of Mary and Joseph to this confirming word? Mary locked up the truth in her heart, and through it received strength for the upbringing of her Child of Promise!

3. *Name your child for purpose.*

   Joseph and Mary obeyed the instructions given by the angel and named the child *Jesus,* which means "Savior," signifying His purpose. A name carries a powerful strength with it. It almost seems that when a child is named, then the spirit of that name receives "legal right" to attach itself to that child.

   Jeremiah, for example, means "hurled, as an arrow" as well as "the exalted one." Jeremiah grew up with a powerful, fearless, and incisive word for his nation! *Jacob* means "usurper." *Jesus Christ* means "the Messiah Savior" and "the Anointed One." The name of my third son is Christopher, "bearer of Christ."

4. *Be willing to suffer yourself.*

   The prophetic word that Simeon spoke over Jesus as He was being presented to the Lord had a tremendous impact upon Mary. *"And Simeon blessed them, and said unto Mary his mother, Behold, this child is set for the fall and rising again of many in Israel; and for a sign which shall be spoken against"* (Luke 2:34).

   Mary must have felt a shock run through her body as she heard the old prophet foretell of opposition that would rise up against her beloved Son. But Simeon wasn't finished yet. Quietly he continued, *"(Yea, a sword shall pierce through thy own soul also)"* (verse 35).

   What a destiny to acknowledge! How could Mary willingly accept this Son who came with a world-shaking purpose and a sword that would pierce her heart? Yet Mary once again *"kept all these sayings in her heart"* (verse 51).

   How would you like to raise a child, and then have Him continually talk about "His Father's business" (Luke 2:49) (when it is clear He's not talking about your business!)? How would you feel if your child said, *"I and my Father are one"* (John 10:30)? Joseph must have felt distanced from this son at times. He knew he had to defer to the One to whom this child had a prior and more intimate allegiance. Many parents are not willing to suffer in this way.

5. *Act quickly to preserve the seed.*

   When King Herod ordered the slaughter of all the innocent male babies in Israel, hoping to destroy the Jewish king he had heard about, Joseph had to act quickly on the words of an angel (Matt. 2). Hurriedly, he took the child and His mother and departed for Egypt. After he received another warning from God in a dream, Joseph returned to live in Galilee because Herod's son was reigning in Judah. God spoke four times to Joseph by dreams. (See Matthew 1–2.)

God has not changed. He still moves to preserve the lives of seeds of promise. Godly parents must stay on guard, alert to every device of the seed-devourer. Just as importantly, they must listen to the warnings and instructions of God and act speedily to preserve their seeds of promise.

6. *Teach your children their heavenly Father's business.*

   Jesus remained in the temple at Jerusalem while His parents began their journey toward home in Nazareth. After a day's travel, they realized that their twelve-year-old was not traveling with their large family group. It was three days before they found Him. That was just the time that Jesus needed! His earthly parents finally found Him dialoguing with the learned men, "*both hearing them* [the spirit of the humble learner], *and asking them questions* [the spirit of the eager inquirer]" (Luke 2:46). Obviously, young Jesus also had an opportunity to speak out, and the result was astonishment at His understanding and answers.

Parenting by Biblical Example

What can we learn from this episode in the lives of Jesus and His earthly parents that will help us raise our own seeds of promise today?

1. *Be gentle and understanding with your sometimes-preoccupied children.* Jesus did not mean to be disobedient. He was totally engrossed in being "about His Father's business."
2. *Teach your children their purpose—their heavenly Father's business.* Teach them and encourage them until it totally occupies their minds and shapes their actions.
3. *Educate your children with God's promises and with the Word of God*
4. *Encourage your children to use their minds and challenge their intelligence.* Use methodology that causes them to ask

questions, to critically evaluate ideas and principles, and to carefully analyze information.

5. *Expect responses like those Jesus gave His parents at the temple. "How is it that ye sought me? wist ye not that I must be about my Father's business?"* (Luke 2:49). When your well-trained children respond to you with these kinds of answers, be prepared to respond, "Yes, for this purpose you were born."
6. *Teach your children to assess their generation.* Children who will become the prophets, priests, and kings of their generation must be aware of the sins of their people and assess their generation.
7. *Teach your children obedience to the will of the Father.* Jesus learned obedience and respect for the law of God very early in His life. He was taught His purpose and shown the prophetic words that outlined His destiny in the Old Testament. Jesus responded to His purpose all of His life: *"For I came...not to do mine own will, but the will of him that sent me"* (John 6:38). *"As my Father hath taught me, I speak these things"* (John 8:28). *"The works that I do in my Father's name"* (John 10:25). *"For I do always those things that please him"* (John 8:29). These were Jesus' responses. Jesus learned obedience, and this was what brought Him to full completion of God's will.

Our heavenly Father can only use the childlike spirit of obedience to fulfill His purposes. Destiny is embedded in the childlike, compliant spirit of the next generation. This is why God invests His promise, purpose, and will in our sons and daughters!

The Two Great Challenges of Godly Parenting

When Mary and Joseph heard the prophetic declaration of their child's destiny, *"He shall save **his people** from their* *sins*" (Matt. 1:21, emphasis added), they faced two tremendous challenges that every godly parent is destined to face:

1. They themselves had to cultivate a deeper love for their nation in their hearts, along with an awareness of the people's need for a deliverer. They would have to give up their child for this nation, and for the entire race of man.
2. They had to commit themselves to depositing their knowledge and love into their Child of Promise. They were responsible for turning the heart of the Child toward His Father and toward the needs His Father had sent Him to meet while He was young. Thus, He would love His nation, see its need, and lay down His life for the deliverance of His people.

Born to Die, Dying to Live

The life of Jesus is a dynamic drama of unbroken sacrifice and commitment to a divine purpose. Jesus Christ was an obedient Son who knew that He was born to die. He looked critically at His generation and accurately assessed its state: "*O faithless and perverse generation,*" and "*evil and adulterous generation*" (Matt. 17:17; 12:39).

This assessment did not spark a long monologue of hatred and self-righteous rejection of His generation. Instead, Jesus expressed His compassion for the lost multitude that wandered about without a shepherd. He tirelessly healed and blessed them. Finally, He even gave up His life for His people.

Raising children of destiny means:

- Making them aware of the needs of their nation.
- Making them aware of the needs of their generation.
- Instilling compassion in their hearts.
- Instilling in them a confidence in their ability to change things for good.

- Telling them, "Child, you were born for such a time as this. You must be a kingly priest for your generation."

Jesus spoke of judgment and delivered eternal salvation. *"Even so shall it be also unto this wicked generation"* (Matt. 12:45). Knowing the judgment of God, Jesus became sin for us and took upon Himself our just punishment for sin, and so brought us salvation. The psalmist wrote, *"A seed shall serve him; it shall be accounted to the Lord for **a generation**"* (Ps. 22:30, emphasis added). Jesus knew that He was the Seed who would atone for the sins of His generation and every generation that would follow it.

Godly Teaching Produces Godly Results

The effects and fruit of Mary and Joseph's covering, teaching, and training were far-reaching. They worked diligently to help Jesus become who and what He was born to be—the Messiah and Savior. Jesus' entire ministry reveals just how well He had learned His lessons.

Jesus' Life Revealed His Early Training

Jesus launched His public ministry in the synagogue in His hometown. He opened the scroll of Isaiah to an ancient prophecy the people had heard countless times in the past.

"The Spirit of the Lord is upon me, because he hath anointed me...he hath sent me to heal the brokenhearted" (Luke 4:18). Rather than finishing the reading, Jesus paused a moment as all eyes were fastened on Him, and then He said, *"This day is this scripture fulfilled in your ears"* (verse 21). Jesus unflinchingly proclaimed His purpose.

Jesus Did Everything with Clarity of Purpose

1. Jesus *knew* the prophetic words spoken concerning Him.
2. Jesus *repeated* the prophetic words spoken concerning Him.

3. Jesus *pulled* those prophetic words into His own experience and made that spiritual word become flesh.
4. Jesus *did* what He was called to do. *"I must preach the kingdom of God to other cities also:* ***for therefore am I sent****"* (Luke 4:43, emphasis added).

Jesus boldly declared His destiny in detail to His disciples. *"Behold, we go up to Jerusalem; and the Son of man shall be betrayed...and they shall condemn him to death...to crucify him: and the third day he shall rise again"* (Matt. 20:18–19).

The night Jesus was betrayed and arrested, He told one of His disciples to put his sword away and said:

> *Thinkest thou that I cannot now pray to my Father, and he shall presently give me more than twelve legions of angels?* ***But how then shall the scriptures be fulfilled, that thus it must be?****...But all this was done, that the scriptures of the prophets might be fulfilled.*
> (Matthew 26:53–54, 56, emphasis added)

Jesus also told His disciples:

> *For these be the days of vengeance, that all things which are written may be fulfilled.* (Luke 21:22)

> *For I say unto you, that this that is written must yet be accomplished in me...* ***for the things concerning me have an end****.* (Luke 22:37, emphasis added)

> *These are the words which I spake unto you, while I was yet with you, that all things must be fulfilled, which were written...concerning me.... Thus it is written, and thus it behoved Christ to suffer, and to rise.* (Luke 24:44, 46)

Jesus knew why He was sent, and He walked purposefully toward His own sacrifice to complete fulfillment. He actively *worked* the prophetic words concerning Him. As parents, we are to do likewise.

What more was needed for Jesus' primary purpose, apart from the fact that it was the will of Father God? God used human instruments—human parents—to be His hands, His feet, and His vehicle to prepare His Son to complete His earthly work. Jesus, the God-Man, brought these earthly complements to His Father's heavenly vision:

1. He *belonged* to a family that pushed Him toward His purpose.
2. He had a *father* who greatly desired the fulfillment of His destiny.
3. He had a *mother* who prodded and instructed Him.
4. He accurately *assessed* His generation.
5. Jesus *wanted* to do His Father's will with all of His heart.
6. Jesus had a consuming desire and unequaled success in *learning the Word and becoming prophetic* in His own life.
7. Jesus "pulled down" prophetic words and intention from eternity and made them become a fulfilled reality on earth. His obedience on earth, in turn, reached up into eternity, and He became the Sacrificed Lamb of God, revealing God's glorious plan from eternity!

Parents' Checklist
Lessons from the Earthly Parents of Jesus

This list of statements will help you evaluate your parental choices in comparison to the lives of Mary and Joseph. First, read the item. Then mark your answer beside each question.

Yes/No

1. I want sons and daughters of promise.
2. I am prepared to disciple and teach them.
3. I am prepared to raise my children and then give them up to God.

Yes/No

4. I am prepared to share the parenthood of my seed with God.

5. I am willing for my children to give their lives for their generation.

6. I believe God will use the children of a humble family like mine.

7. I am prepared to bear the pain of loneliness and separation from my children if necessary.

8. I know I have heard the word of promise for my child.

9. I have already said, *"Be it unto me according to thy word"* (Luke 1:38).

10. I see myself as a generational link.

11. I remember every word of promise God has ever given me for my children.

12. I have given my children names that have purpose in their meaning.

13. I am willing to suffer and do whatever is necessary for my children to fulfill their calling.

14. I am always alert and act speedily for my children's preservation.

15. I teach my children their "Father's business."

16. I am very careful in my treatment of my children of promise.

17. I teach my children to ask questions and to critically evaluate and carefully analyze things.

18. I teach my children to assess their generation and the state of the people. My children will already know or will be taught the needs of their nation.

Yes/No

19. My children are learning obedience to the will of their Father.

20. My children already know or are learning their purpose.

21. My children are learning to purposefully do what God said they would.

Review your responses to these statements and identify the area(s) that you are still working on. Then make a plan to help you raise your children to fulfill God's purpose and intention for their lives.

Problems Parents Have

There are a number of pitfalls and misconceptions that cause parents to miss the mark as generational links and collaborators with God's purpose.

1. We hold on to the anointings we receive and are unwilling to pass them on to our children. The truth is that we are unwilling to "die" so that our children may live.
2. We have no future vision for our personal ministries. Thus, by word and deed, we blunt our children's vision and potential.
3. When the children cry, "Where is the God of our fathers?", we ask the same question and start looking for the answer when we should already know it. We should be pointing our children to our God.
4. We are unwilling to build up our children, and sometimes we are even unwilling to call our children by our name. Absalom, the rebellious son of David, raised up a memorial pillar for himself, and said, *"I have no son to keep my name in remembrance: and he called the pillar after his own name: and it is called unto this day, Absalom's place"* (2 Sam. 18:18).

Absalom later died in a rebellion against his own father; he was killed while hanging in a tree (2 Sam. 18:9–15). Children help keep our names in remembrance, which is an honorable goal.

5. We literally abort our own heritage through our inability and unwillingness to invest in the next generation. King Saul cursed his son, Jonathan, *"For as long as the son of Jesse liveth upon the ground, thou shalt not be established, nor thy kingdom"* (1 Sam. 20:31). Out of fear and jealousy, this man cursed his own seed.

6. We bring death to our seed in the following ways:

   a. Onanism—We are unwilling to bring forth seed and collaborate with God in building His kingdom (Gen. 38:9).

   b. Abortion—We believe the lies of the enemy or become so selfish that we kill our own seed and become our own seed-devourers.

   c. Evil training—The mother of Sisera waited for her beloved son to come home with the spoils of war that she coveted (Judg. 4; 5:28–30). This son, who had oppressed Israel for twenty years, finally met defeat at the hands of God. Instead of returning home with the spoils of war his mother had become fond of, Sisera, the mighty captain, was killed by a woman and received his just reward. His mother's sadness is the same as that of all the parents who fail to restrain their children from wrongdoing.

   d. Our own breaking of covenants—God told the priests of Malachi's day, *"I will corrupt your seed"* (Mal. 2:3). They had broken marriage covenants as well as priestly and brotherly covenants. God had to intervene and put an end to their abominable priesthood by chastising their seed.

   e. Our careless lack of guidance and control—Eli's sons suffered early death, and God's priestly gift was removed because Eli did not restrain his sons from evil-doing, and also because Eli honored his sons above God (1 Sam. 2).

f. Our blatant sinfulness (Hos. 4:6–7)—Sinfulness can cause both parents and children to be destroyed. *"Seeing thou hast forgotten the law of thy God, I will also forget thy children"* (Hos. 4:6). *"And I will not have mercy upon her children; for they be the children of whoredoms"* (Hos. 2:4). *"The mother was dashed in pieces upon her children"* (Hos. 10:14).

g. Our sinful living—This brings a curse of cannibalistic practices. They will *"eat the flesh of their sons and the flesh of their daughters"* (Jer. 19:9). This implies a reckless feasting on the property and rights of children by parents, whose very behavior leads to famine or the wrath of God.

h. Our enmity against God and His people—This brings death to our children. Of Ahab it was said, *"For the whole house of Ahab shall perish"* (2 Kings 9:8). *"And Ahab had seventy sons in Samaria....They took the king's sons, and slew seventy persons, and put their heads in baskets"* (2 Kings 10:1, 7). The curses upon fathers fall upon their ensuing generations.

7
The Roles and Rights of Fathers

There are many lessons to be learned from the Bible story of a prominent Jewish family. It is a story of success, transference, and succession. It is one that displays the role of parents, their partnership with children in fulfilling destiny, and the benefits that result when parents provide for their children.

David, the son of Jesse, belonging to the tribe of Judah, was born during the reign of Saul, whose rulership was typified by ruthless principles and ungodly practices. It was time for God's intervention.

The history of a nation, God's chosen people, was coming to a radical turning point. God ceaselessly searched and probed for men and women who would bear children of promise. The Almighty found such a man in David. This man was not perfect, but he exhibited traits and characteristics that should mark responsible parents of every generation:

1. David was willing to collaborate with God in birthing and raising children of purpose.
2. David desired to prolong his life and extend his purpose into the next generation through his children. David had

long-range plans for his children, in the same way a kingdom usually doesn't end when there is a successor.

3. David's plans for his children were more far-reaching than those for his own reign and kingship. His promise to Bathsheba was that Solomon would reign in his stead (1 Kings 1:17). God had already told David that he would have a son of rest who would one day establish the throne of God's kingdom over Israel.

   Solomon's name means "rest" or "comfort." He was the second son of David and Bathsheba, and his mother's only surviving son (although his father had many sons through various wives). Solomon's birth and life reminded his parents (and the public) of David's lustful concupiscence and willful murder of his mother's first husband.

   Could anything good and godly come out of this conjugal relationship? Would the power of God's will bypass the seemingly lustful and prideful will of Solomon's father? How powerfully at work was God's divine intention and purpose for David's son? And how much did David want his son to complete the work he had started?

David Made Strategic Plans

The life of Solomon, David's son of promise, illustrates the outworking of God's will in a child's life through the strategic planning of a father.

Early in Solomon's life, David detected that his son had the ability and character to be the next king. David carefully programmed his son for future kingship. He patiently invested in Solomon all of the wisdom, knowledge, and understanding that his own experience had taught him. The proverbs of Solomon are a lasting tribute to lessons he was taught by his wise father and mother.

Three thousand proverbs of wisdom and more than one thousand songs poured from the heart and pen of David's son Solomon. All of these had their source in the heart and the lips of David, Bathsheba, and carefully selected teachers designated by Solomon's parents. Later, Solomon repeatedly taught his sons and other young men, *"My son, hear the instruction of thy father, and forsake not the law of thy mother"* (Prov. 1:8).

A well-learned truth on the lips of a son is striking evidence of the patient and wise teaching of a father who is perceptive and determined to seize every opportunity for the good of his children. This father measures his actions toward his children by the thought, "I must rear these children for greatness." The wise father knows that godly wisdom will preserve his child and provide the tools needed to preserve his children's generation.

Fathers who possess wisdom will reason, "My children will lead men, so their abilities must surpass those of others. They must love their people and want to see them make wise choices and decisions. I will teach them to discern the way of the world. I will also teach them to mark well the actions and demands of a God of mercy and justice." It was under this kind of instruction that Solomon grew in stature, wisdom, and the knowledge of God. Solomon grew to manhood and his father's throne because of his parents' purposeful, premeditated, and carefully planned collaboration with God. David and Bathsheba sought partnership with God in bearing a child of purpose.

David Heard God's Purpose for Solomon

The Bible records God's plan for David's posterity in excellent precision and detail in the book of 1 Chronicles. God's amazing reaction to this man who was willing to "establish," or build, Him a house was that God Himself would build or establish David's house and kingdom.

> *I tell thee that the LORD will build thee an house. And it shall come to pass, when thy days be expired that thou must*

> *go to be with thy fathers, that I will raise up thy seed after thee, which shall be of thy sons; and I will establish his kingdom. He shall build me an house, and I will stablish his throne for ever. I will be his father, and he shall be my son: and I will not take my mercy away from him, as I took it from him that was before thee.* (1 Chron. 17:10–13)

God is always the "Senior Partner." The work of the spirit of purpose and destiny is not to be outdone. Even the best father can never outdo God when it comes to planning for the future establishment of God's kingdom. God said, "[I] *will build thee an house...I will raise up thy seed after thee...I will stablish his throne for ever*" (1 Chron. 17:10–12).

Did you notice how clearly God's deep-seated desire and plan appeared in His prophecy to David? He was personal and possessive in the best sense: *"I will be his father, and he shall be my son"* (1 Chron. 17:13). God is vitally interested in fathering children. He is always seeking out His divine heritage by "adopting" the children of men whose loins bring forth children of purpose and whose hearts are determined to establish God's name and kingdom.

In this passage in 1 Chronicles, we witness the exchange of a covenant between a man and his God. David the man said, "God, I am willing to build Your house." God the Father replied, "Beloved earthly father, I will build your house. I will do it by raising up your seed after you. I will establish his house forever!" Such is the covenant of an eternal Father God on behalf of children! He gave to David a promise that his seed would be blessed forever.

This type of covenant exchange is also found in the book of Psalms. *"I will sing of the mercies of the LORD for ever: with my mouth will I make known thy faithfulness to all generations"* (Ps. 89:1). The God of covenant always responds to "generational" men and women with a promise to bless their seed: *"Thy seed will I establish for ever, and build up thy throne to all generations.*

Selah" (Ps. 89:4). And again, *"What man is he that feareth the LORD? him shall he teach in the way that he shall choose. His soul shall dwell at ease; and his seed shall inherit the earth"* (Ps. 25:12–13).

God searches and waits for fathers who will express their willingness to teach and bless ensuing generations and who will make covenant with their Father God for children of promise!

A Father's Prayer

David not only heard God's expression of His divine intention for his son Solomon—he also prayed *publicly* that God's purpose would be fulfilled!

> *Therefore now, LORD, let the thing that thou hast spoken concerning thy servant and concerning his house be established for ever, and do as thou hast said. Let it even be established, that thy name may be magnified for ever, saying, The LORD of hosts is the God of Israel, even a God to Israel: and let the house of David thy servant be established before thee. For thou, O my God, hast told thy servant that thou wilt build him an house: therefore thy servant hath found in his heart to pray before thee. And now, LORD, thou art God, and hast promised this goodness unto thy servant: Now therefore let it please thee to bless the house of thy servant, that it may be before thee for ever: for thou blessest, O LORD, and it shall be blessed for ever.* (1 Chron. 17:23–27)

David had a spirit that understood eternity. He was generous and long-term in his thinking. He could stretch himself into the future and make petitions, plans, and provisions for that future.

His most outstanding statement was at once a request and an oath. David asked God to do whatever He wanted to do and swore that he would do his part in the divine transaction.

David's earnest prayer for a blessing for his son is an example to every godly parent. "*Therefore now,* LORD, *let the thing that thou hast spoken concerning thy servant and concerning his house be established for ever, and do as thou hast said*" (1 Chron. 17:23). David did not sit back and simply wait for his omnipotent God's stated will to be executed. He prayed God's will into existence in the earth! This is the task of every parent who co-labors with God.

A Father's Plea

Study David's reaction after he heard the prophet outline God's intention and plan to bless Solomon.

> *And David the king came and sat before the* LORD, *and said, Who am I, O* LORD *God, and what is mine house, that thou hast brought me hitherto?...For thou hast also spoken of thy servant's house for a great while to come....And what one nation in the earth is like thy people Israel....For thy people Israel didst thou make thine own people for ever.*
> (1 Chron. 17:16–17, 21–22)

"Why was my family and house chosen? Why are these multi-generational promises being made for my family? Why has my people, my nation, been chosen for this special honor?"

David "*came and sat before the* LORD" and began to speak to Him. This reveals the significance David attached to this matter. He also had many questions for God: "Who am I, and why did You choose me? Why did You choose my house? Why did You select my son for furthering Your purposes on the earth?" David's questions demonstrated his humble acceptance of the call on his family and seed.

It is significant that David recognized that his call—and that of his children—was for the benefit of his nation. He had literally extended his own vision by aligning it with the far-reaching vision of an eternal God. David was humbled by

God's promise to make his kingly office endure forever among his descendants, for he clearly knew there was no guarantee it would happen otherwise. Proverbs 27:24 says, *"For riches are not for ever: and doth the crown endure to every generation?"* David ascended to the throne solely by God's supreme choice! His sin of adultery with Bathsheba, as well as the murder of her husband, militated against his continued rulership over Israel as God's chosen leader.

God is clearly willing to bless kings with a *generational anointing* for their seed to inherit kingship. His perfect plan and divine economy is for children to inherit their fathers' accumulated wisdom, blessing, anointing, and responsibility from generation to generation. Wise Solomon was but one example of a father successfully transferring much of his wisdom, anointing, and earthly power into the hands of his son.

What would happen if we today could successfully transfer our anointing, our faith, our righteousness, our vision, and our earthly possessions into the hands of three or four generations of our seed? The answer is simple: Our seed would inherit the earth!

David Sealed His Son's Blessing

David "sealed" the word of the Lord for his seed with a prayer agreement with God. This prayer sealed his son's blessing and calling: *"Therefore now, LORD, let the thing that thou hast spoken concerning thy servant and concerning his house be established for ever, and do as thou hast said"* (1 Chron. 17:23). David's prayer accepted and sealed God's promise, thereby placing the responsibility for the performance of the blessing back in God's hands. God is still searching for fathers in our generation who are willing to do as David did. Like David, we should approach our Lord with humility, thanksgiving, and total confidence in His Word. We need to recognize that

God's eternal desire is to be merciful (1 Chron. 17:13) and to establish His kingdom (1 Chron. 17:23). He has sovereignly chosen to covenant with man for seed of promise. It is through our seed that God intends to reveal and express His eternal nature in the generations of man.

David also consummated the covenant with the words, *"Let the thing that thou hast spoken concerning thy servant and concerning his house be established for ever, and do as thou hast said"* (1 Chron. 17:23).

David Gave a Charge to His Son

David understood his responsibility well. He followed a pattern that we should also follow. First, David knew the high calling of God on his son's life, and he understood the seriousness of the purpose of God. As a man in authority, he had learned much about the delegation of duty and how proper lines of authority must be followed. For these reasons, David called Solomon before a group of witnesses and publicly charged or imposed the responsibility of his God-given assignment and task upon him.

> *Then he called for Solomon his son, and charged him to build an house for the LORD God of Israel. And David said to Solomon, My son, as for me, it was in my mind to build an house unto the name of the LORD my God: but the word of the LORD came to me, saying, Thou hast shed blood abundantly, and hast made great wars: thou shalt not build an house unto my name, because thou hast shed much blood upon the earth in my sight. Behold, a son shall be born to thee, who shall be a man of rest; and I will give him rest from all his enemies round about: for his name shall be Solomon, and I will give peace and quietness unto Israel in his days. He shall build an house for my name; and he shall be my son, and I will be his father; and I will establish the throne of his kingdom over Israel for ever. Now, my son, the*

LORD be with thee; and prosper thou, and build the house of the LORD thy God, as he hath said of thee. Only the LORD give thee wisdom and understanding, and give thee charge concerning Israel, that thou mayest keep the law of the LORD thy God. (1 Chron. 22:6–12)

Certain pivotal words stand out as those of a man who seriously declares to his son a solemn charge. David charged Solomon to build a house for the Lord God. After repeating to Solomon God's intention to use him, David said, ***"Now, my son**...build the house"* (1 Chron. 22:11, emphasis added). Later, after blessing him, David told Solomon, *"Arise therefore, and be doing"* (1 Chron. 22:16).

David's Prayer and Blessing

David was a good father who foresaw the need for his son to have great wisdom and understanding. That is why he wisely prayed, *"Only the LORD give thee wisdom and understanding"* (1 Chron. 22:12). Many people teach that Solomon alone was responsible for seeking God for wisdom. However, this passage clearly shows that the gift of wisdom granted by God to Solomon was precipitated by a prayer from a father's heart. (That was a prayer that God heard and answered.) David earnestly prayed, *"And give unto Solomon my son a perfect heart"* (1 Chron. 29:19).

David Provided for His Son's Destiny

King David wasn't satisfied with simply sitting by while his son grew up to fulfill some future destiny. He immediately began gathering resources and information to help his son fulfill his purpose when the time came. His provision came in several areas:

1. David provided materials for his son. As a wise father, David *anticipated* his son's needs. He assembled and organized all of the building materials Solomon would

need to build the house of the Lord God. He provided the gold, the silver, the brass, and the timber. He even arranged with his allies and neighboring trade partners to provide rare specialty materials, workmen, and skilled craftsmen (1 Kings 7:40–45).

2. Solomon's father also provided complete administrative support for his future task. *"David also commanded all the princes of Israel to help Solomon his son"* (1 Chron. 22:17). He also organized their donations (1 Chron. 29:1–9).
3. The king provided for the priestly support his son would need. David meticulously prepared the temple workers, the priests, and all other workers in advance *"for the service of the house of the LORD"* (1 Chron. 23–25). Keep in mind that there had never been a temple before this time.
4. David provided a divine pattern for Solomon to follow. What a father! David did not permit his son to flounder about helplessly, learning by trial and error. The things of God require expertise, precision, and purpose. *"Then David gave to Solomon his son...the pattern of all that he had by the spirit, of the courts of the house of the LORD"* (1 Chron. 28:11–12). David passed on to his son all that the Lord had revealed to him! Did you notice that it was not given grudgingly? It was lavishly, fully, and generously passed on to his seed for the next generation.
5. David passed his authority on to Solomon. The final stage of David's preparation was to formally and publicly affirm his delegation of authority and kingly leadership to Solomon before all of his princes, priests, Levites, and the assembled congregation of Israel. He declared that his son was called by God for the task: *"Solomon my son, whom alone God hath chosen"* (1 Chron. 29:1). As a result, everyone present knew that the king had instructed Solomon that *"the princes and all the people will be wholly*

at thy commandment" (1 Chron. 28:21). The result was that David's son began his task with every necessary provision apart from his own obedience to God: "*And all the princes, and the mighty men, and all the sons likewise of king David, submitted themselves unto Solomon the king*" (1 Chron. 29:24).

Collaboration with God Produces Results

David's obedient collaboration with God produced the wisest son in the earth, increased his nation's strength and influence, helped build a temple for God, and fulfilled God's purpose in bringing the Messiah to earth through his seed.

It was because of godly training and mentoring that "*the Lord magnified Solomon exceedingly in the sight of all Israel*" (1 Chron. 29:25). It was the countless hours and years of instruction about the importance of destiny and vision that caused David's son to pray these words on his day of coronation, "*Now, O Lord God, let thy promise unto David my father be established*" (2 Chron. 1:9).

This is the vital circle of life that guarantees God's blessing: God proposes to a father, who blesses his children and raises them accordingly. The children then reiterate before God the promise He made to their father, and God moves into action to perform His predetermined will.

Solomon's prayer for wisdom in 2 Chronicles 1:10 exactly matched the desire and prayer of his father in 1 Chronicles 22:12. For that reason, God granted Solomon wisdom and much more! (See 1 Chronicles 1:12.)

Charge to the Fathers of Promised Seed

1. Dare to dream for the future. Dream for your children and your children's children.

2. Dare to have visions. Put yourself into the future, into God's eternal now, and see with His eyes what He has laid up for your sons and daughters.
3. Have a daring fearlessness, a godly confidence that the future will not overwhelm you. Know that your children and their children will have the power, strength, giftings, and authority to do more than what you can do. They will arise in their generation as fearless executors of God's will and purpose.
4. Dare to believe that this world has a chance at survival because your children have the high calling of God on their lives, and that means rulership, priesthood, and the power of God's Word on their lips.
5. Dare to believe that the history of your nation is wrapped up in the blessing that you have bestowed on your children today!
6. Dare to approach God's presence with your strong petitions and frequent reminders of His promises. God longs for fathers who will dare to come to Him to dialogue about their children and His seed.
7. Dare to speak and declare directive words of prophetic intention for your children with the mind of Christ and the heart of God, with sonship in your own spirit and priesthood and rulership in your own soul. (The Father awaits the maturing of all of His children, so they will stand alongside Him and assume true parenthood.) Realize the power of your spoken word.
8. Speak to the people who will be supportive of what your children have responsibility for.
9. Provide generously and lavishly for your children and for what they have been called to do.
10. Remember the oath and the promises you made!

True fatherhood necessarily implies the right to organize for the salvation of the race through its children.

Parents' Checklist
Raising Young Leaders: The Example of David

First read the item. Then mark "Yes" or "No."

Yes/No

1. I recognize that my children's births were not accidents.
2. I listen carefully to God's plan for my children.
3. I am willing to collaborate with God on behalf of my people.
4. I see God's kingdom being established by my children in the next generation.
5. I am willing to extend my own purpose into and through the life of my children.
6. I look closely at my children for the character traits of prophets, priests, or kings.
7. I "program" or train and teach my children to become the prophets, priests, and kings of their generation.
8. I teach my children to love their nation.
9. I observe my children's growth in stature, wisdom, and the knowledge of God.
10. I pronounce blessings on my children in my home.
11. I publicly pronounce blessings on my children.
12. I am willing to make a covenant with God for my children.
13. I pray earnestly to God for His promise to come to pass.

Yes/No

14. I pray God's will into existence in the life of my children.

15. I realize that God's choice is sovereign.

16. I seriously and solemnly charge my children with God's call.

17. I provide financially for my children's future call.

18. I provide administrative support for my children's future calls.

19. I provide the pattern and the know-how for my children to complete God's work in the God-given and prescribed way.

20. I declare my children's authority among the leaders of the people.

21. I watch to see God increasing and blessing my children.

22. I watch to see God's out-working of His gifts in my children.

23. I watch to see God's promises come to pass.

24. I listen for my children's personal requests to God for wisdom.

25. I watch for God's beautiful answer in my children's fulfillment of purpose!

Review your answers and identify the areas where you still have to wait for affirmative answers. Begin now to plan your own strategies as you collaborate with God to bless and prepare your children for the fulfillment of their eternal purpose.

8
Molding the Minds of Leaders

Every ungodly government and social order that has risen to power in history has understood what the church and many parents have not: There is power in the children. Hitler knew the secret of the seed. He mobilized the zeal, energy, and boundless optimism of Germany's youth and launched a world war with the fire they started. Communist governments around the world have been quick to separate the young from their parents so they could carefully mold the children's impressionable minds for their own purposes. Parents have been warned and reminded about the importance of our children. When we see only our young and perhaps "headstrong" children, God sees mighty leaders doing great exploits in His name. It is time for us to wake up and see as God sees. Our future is at stake.

One of the greatest weaknesses I see in Christian books on child-rearing is a profound lack of specific, practical guidelines or directives to help parents "get the job done right." Since we agree that we need to raise our children to fulfill God's purposes in their generation, now we must ask, "What should we teach them, and how should we do it?" There are seven broad areas of knowledge in which our children must receive instruction:

1. Every child needs a solid general education. It should be based on time-tested principles.
2. Children need to know who they are in Christ Jesus and how they can properly appropriate every blessing God has promised them.
3. Children must learn how to personally discover the purpose of God for their lives.
4. No child can fulfill his God-ordained destiny unless he learns from his parents how to hear the voice of God and discern truth.
5. Children of destiny must learn to hear or perceive the needs of their people and the people of the world. They must be taught to love their people.
6. Children need to develop a life of self-government and discipline so that they will not waste their God-given talents. If a child can rule his own spirit, he will learn to rule his household and later his community.
7. Children must be taught how to live without fear and greed. They will grow to make a difference in nations ruled by corrupt men and systems.

General Education and Training for Giftedness

The basic foundation for our children's growth and achievement is their cognitive and intellectual development. They need to learn how to think, discern, and decide. Our children need healthy minds as well as healthy spirits.

The ability to think—to analyze and conceptualize, and to reason—is one of the most important gifts we received through Adam. It is one of the most dynamic ways that we reflect God's likeness and image. God is the supreme intelligent One, and we are intelligent beings after His divine pattern. Consider these important points about the general education of our children:

1. *Pre-birth preparation:* Education begins even before birth! Even while your child is still in the womb, he or she will be heavily influenced by external factors, including a sense of acceptance or rejection and of security or insecurity. Both fathers and mothers are responsible for providing a positive atmosphere for prenatal development.

   Mothers: Be conscious of the fact that what you are is what goes into your baby. Toxic glandular secretions brought about by stress and anxiety will cross the uterine walls and the placenta. When these toxins penetrate into your baby's body, they have a much greater toxic effect on the baby than they have on you!

   Stimulate your children *in utero* (while they are still in the womb). Various medical reports indicate that listening to good music, giving thanks and having a joyful heart, reading the Word, and singing to a baby in the womb have an intellectually enriching effect on his or her mind. Some mothers even report that their children had early acquisition of number and reading skills after they were exposed to readiness concepts such as number concepts and vowel sounds while still in the womb.

   Most important of all: Mothers, prepare your child to have a sound mind by taking care of your body throughout your pregnancy. Guard your health and preserve a gentle, rich, and strong spirit.

2. *Newborn preparation:* Prepare your newborn for greatness. Begin to foster all that is necessary for a healthy body, soul, and spirit in your newborn. This includes providing nutritious food and a sense of warmth, comfort, and security; verbally communicating with your baby at every opportunity; and providing age-appropriate

environmental stimulation. I recommend that you seek wise counsel concerning when to introduce more formal learning to your child. Remember, however, that God has made your child in *His image.* Your child has a fantastic untapped ability to learn. You, the parent, are—and always will be—his primary teacher. Your child's intellectual development will most likely outstrip your expectations. Aim high (staying within reasonable and God-given limits), and your child will reach your expectations and most likely surpass them.

Remember that important *readiness* stage where informal learning plays such a major role. Cultivate a desire in your child to achieve, to learn, and to listen to new ideas. Develop an inquiring spirit in your baby through games and verbal communication. Teach your child to stack and sort, to open and close, to go up and to come down as you spend time with your child early in his life. This early abstract manipulation of concepts creates a rich readiness base for your child's cognitive development.

3. *Communication and information processing development:* Answer your child's questions—yes, even those repeated questions! Wait for a reply and then ask your child questions in turn. Expect and probe for a logical and suitable answer from your child (an answer that you would reasonably expect from a child of his age). Note: Remember that your child is watching and listening. Be sure to label and name items properly, describe events with clarity, and thus teach your child above-average verbal skills.

   Look for small ways to teach your children the importance of accuracy and efficiency. Teach them the value of "doing it just right" every time and train them to expect good results. This skill forms the basis for mathematical prowess later.

Provide suitable materials for your child to manipulate to help develop basic concepts of how things fit together and how physical laws and principles work. Let him learn that he is the manipulator and he can control variables within his reach. This is leadership training.

Warning: I have discovered that weak and sluggish communication on the part of parents produces a far more negative effect on a child's learning acquisition than any shortage of materials to learn from. Yes, children need a listening ear, an encouraging smile, and a helpful hand. However, they also thrive on a precise answer, a probing question, a ready wit, and an environment where they can explore their own creativity and seek truth.

4. *Formal education for your young leader:* Provide your school-aged child with the best possible formal education available. You may choose between homeschooling, private Christian schools, or public schools. Again, remember that you are—and always will be—your child's best teacher. Make radical changes to your life-style to facilitate your child's education if necessary.

   Invest the most you can in the best that you have—your children. Compare various curricula, combine them, and expertly carve out a program of learning that is suitable for your child's specific needs. Set your goals high, not so much to compete with others, but to prepare your child for assuming his God-given responsibilities. (Remember to take time to reflect on your triumphs and shared experiences. Enjoy your children now.)

Notes on the Parent/School Relationship

Ah! What a busy parent you must still continue to be!

Daily contact with school and teacher.

Avid study of the classroom curriculum.

Unending and close scrutiny of what your child is learning,

And greater scrutiny of who is teaching your child.

A working relationship with all school personnel,

A willingness to pitch in to help at school,

Daily questioning of all caregivers, "How did my child do today?"

Probing questions and action if something seems out of place for your child's body of knowledge.

Remember—it's your child and your primary responsibility. (Don't leave it to the church, and certainly not to the state.)

Choose your child's school carefully (unless you have chosen to homeschool your child). Choose a school that operates in a true partnership role with you as the parent.

a. Is the central aim of the school's philosophy to lead your child to Jesus Christ?

b. Are the teachers and staff members godly men and women of exemplary Christlike character?

c. Is the curriculum Bible-based, developed on sound time-tested values and principles, and are the individual courses built on those biblical principles? Watch carefully for the intrusion of secular humanistic philosophy in all material, in both subject matter and methodology. Seek expert advice if necessary.

d. Does the administrator or principal put a major emphasis on high academic achievement?

e. Are the school guidelines for good conduct and obedience designed to help each student build a covenant love relationship with God? (Or are they merely punitive measures with no capacity to draw a student closer to God?)

f. Does the administrative and teaching staff view their students as unique individuals created in God's image?

Do they believe and serve as if each student has great individual potential and a unique purpose in his or her generation?

g. Is balanced attention paid to the development of spirit, soul, and body in areas such as athletic and social development?

5. *Parent/Teacher Relationship:* Perhaps the most important key to your child's progress and education in a school setting is your relationship with your child! These guidelines may help you develop this critical area.

   a. Maintain a constant vigil over your child's ongoing courses of study and subject matter.

   b. Ask questions every day concerning your child's state of well-being.

   c. Willingly help your child with homework and preparatory work. Always be ready to study or read with your child. Always be available to discuss things with your child. (It is a wonderful experience for a parent to be the first to introduce a child to a new concept!)

   d. Probe continually so you can discern any potential learning problems at an early stage when they can be more easily corrected. Ask God for this spiritual gift of discernment. Search your local library shelves for reference books and visit secondhand bookshops to satisfy your child's natural insatiable desire to read.

   e. Dig up the books that Grandma and Grandpa read when they were children—the old classics and the phonics reading books. They will probably do you more good than the "improved and modernized" texts currently being used.

   f. Remember that it is more important to teach courage than to simply make a difficult job or assignment easy for your child.

g. It is more important to teach your child perseverance than to supply an easy way out.

h. Teach your child confidence. It is more enduring than parental overprotection.

i. Teach your child patience. It is more gracious than parental overindulgence.

j. Above all, teach your child to love generously, to give freely, to show mercy bountifully, to share himself selflessly. Teach him to walk humbly with his God and to stand tall and strong among his peers!

Important Lessons for Young Students and Leaders

I have provided a number of lists in this book, but each list contains unique elements especially tailored for a specific task. This quick list highlights some of the important lessons in wisdom, knowledge, and understanding your children need to learn to fully inherit God's promises.

1. Teach the way of the Lord. (See Deuteronomy 6:1–2.) If you don't, they will not prosper, and neither will you.
2. Teach obedience to the way of the Lord (Deut. 6:25; 7:9–12). *"And that their children, which have not known any thing, may hear, and learn to fear the LORD your God, as long as ye live in the land whither ye go over Jordan to possess it"* (Deut. 31:13). The spirit of obedience is what your child gains as he builds a relationship with his Father God.
3. Teach absolutes. Our children are being bombarded with a relativistic and secular education that does not teach God's holy law or present basic enduring principles.
4. Teach the difference between the holy and the profane (Heb. 5:14). Teach this from the earliest year through adulthood. Your young child needs to have a natural ability to "smell" a lie, to know what's ungodly, and to discern the counterfeit from the real.

5. Teach your children to have truth *"in the inward parts"* (Ps. 51:6). Don't accept white lies and half-truths. Insist on truth, or you will open up your child to a spirit of deception and a life of shame.
6. Teach God's law and truth as the supreme authority. It is not what you say, it is what God's Word says!
7. Teach your children to offer acceptable sacrifices (Gen. 4:4). Why did Cain fail to offer God an acceptable sacrifice? Cain knew exactly what God required for sacrifices but he was spoiled and petulant in his attitude. First he was disobedient, then stubborn, then rebellious, and finally he was murderous! Always refer to God's law as you remind children of what God expects.
8. Teach dominion and authority (Gen. 1:28). Don't let your children walk around not knowing their place in God and the potential He has given to them.
9. Teach your children the value of work (Gen. 2:15). Work is not a curse. It predated the fall of man in the garden! It is a blessing given for man to attain his true potential.
10. Teach your children to hear, discern, and heed the voice of God. A very young child can practice this. Tell the child, "Go to your room and listen to what Jesus will tell you." The Holy Spirit is always waiting to speak.
11. Teach your children how to grow in knowledge, understanding, and wisdom.
12. Teach your children the fear of the Lord. Without this healthy fear and respect, your children have the unhealthy fear of man. The Bible says this brings a snare (Prov. 29:25)! Teach your children to submit to God's holiness and sovereignty and teach them to be willing to walk in God's way.
13. Teach your children their purpose. Tell them what God has purposed for them.

14. Teach your children leadership skills for nation building. Your children are the prophets, priests, and kings of the future—they were born to transform their generation. All educational programming must center around your children's calls in God. The nation needs the godliness of your seed. Your seed has God's heart, God's law, and God's love for the people and the nation. They must be trained for leadership!
15. Teach your children who they are in Christ Jesus. Teach them to paraphrase and personalize key "identity" Scriptures and confess or rehearse them to renew their minds daily and prepare them for leadership (Rom. 12:2). For example:

    a. Christ dwells in my heart (Eph. 3:17).

    b. God has given me a name like the name of the great men who are in the earth (1 Chron. 17:8).

    c. I am made in the image of God (Gen. 1:27).

    d. God is my Father and I am His child (1 Chron. 17:13).

    e. God is my Maker who gives me songs in the night (Job 35:10).

    f. I will wait on the Lord and be of good courage, and He will strengthen my heart (Ps. 27:14).

    g. I will praise God, for I am fearfully and wonderfully made (Ps. 139:14).

    h. I give thanks always for all things unto God the Father (Eph. 5:20a).

    i. God has raised me up and made me to sit together with Him in heavenly places in Christ Jesus (Eph. 2:6).

    j. God gives me knowledge and skills in all learning and wisdom (Dan. 1:17).

Every day and in the night hours, plant the Word of God into your children of destiny. When they are young, read God's

Word to them. Speak it to them as you bathe or feed your children. Teach them to affirm themselves, "I am a child of God, and God's eyes follow me everywhere I go." This will help your children become filled with the presence and knowledge of God, and they will know who they are in Him and why they were created.

Your children need to learn who their heavenly Father is. Introduce them early to the God of their fathers. God says, *"And when thy son asketh thee in time to come...Then thou shalt say unto thy son..."* (Deut. 6:20–21). God is telling parents, "Show Me off to your children. Brag about My mighty deeds on your behalf. Tell them how well I have provided for their fathers before them. Teach them that I am still the same, and reassure them that for their fathers' sake, I will bless them!" God's blessings, confirmed by oath to fathers, will be given to their seed. This is their heritage.

We should "build altars" and "erect testimonials" to God's hand of providence and victory in our lives. Later, when our children ask, "What do these altars mean?" we can tell them about God. *"And it shall be when thy son asketh thee in time to come, saying, What is this? that thou shalt say unto him, By strength of hand the LORD brought us out from Egypt, from the house of bondage"* (Exod. 13:14). Repeat to your children old family victories, the history of your family's deliverance, and the good gifts granted to you. Boast of the victories you have experienced.

Continually make a record of God's dealings with you, and seize every opportunity to testify to your children of God's strength and power. Establish God's unfailing love from generation to generation. Tell your children, "God was faithful to my father. He is faithful to me. And He will do the same for you and for your children. He is the God of our fathers!"

The best way for a child to learn to become a follower of God is to see his or her own father living as a son of God. A father can instill more in his children than a thousand lessons on "sonship" simply by openly and consistently displaying his reverence for God, his friendship and communication with God, his awe of God, and his obvious submission and obedience to God. Don't stop after you have introduced your children to your heavenly Father. Teach them to walk in your footsteps, and enjoy the Father together.

Teach Your Children to Know the God of the Word

Is it important to teach children God's law? Yes, it is very important! Is it important to teach children the importance of obedience? Yes, it certainly is! *But it is more important to introduce a child to his Father and to help him develop a covenant love relationship with his Savior.* It is out of that relationship with God that your children will naturally, easily, and willingly please the Father by loving obedience.

Help Your Children to Commune with God

1. Develop your own relationship with the Father. Your children should awake in the morning hearing you talk to Him. Your children should see a glow on your face as you come out of a close encounter with God. They should hear you spontaneously whisper, "O God, how good You are to me!"
2. Your children should learn respect for God's Word as they witness your reverent and constant reference to God's Word and law.
3. When giving children a command or rule, or even wise counsel, always base it on God's Word. "God's Word says" and, "God the Father has placed me in charge of you" and then, "Now this is what I want you to do." Consequently, obedience to you becomes natural obedience to your God. In this way, obedience brings joyful—not painful—submission to God that will outlive a young child's imposed obedience to a powerful Father.

Any time a father makes a mistake in disobedience to God's Word and reaps God's just recompense, his children can learn from their father's mistake, just as they learn from his obedience. This is the way children learn the truth of Deuteronomy 28: Obedience brings blessings, but disobedience brings curses. A child will learn to trust God's faithfulness, and his security will be in the fact that God is always true to His Word.

As a father obeys God's Word and reaps His promised blessings, so will his children learn that their father's God is both just and gracious and that a covenant God always keeps His Word. Live your faith before your children, and they will learn to trust in your covenant God. In addition, your children will automatically learn, for example, how to acquire wealth, how to have a long life, and how to walk in divine health.

Generational Discipleship and Instruction

The powerful testimony of generational discipleship and instruction presented in Psalm 78:2–11 first gives the principle and then offers a sad example of what happened when children forgot to apply that principle.

It is the story of a people who were taught how to fight to win battles and who won supernatural victories using their well-learned lessons. They were cautioned to teach their children these principles of warfare, along with the faith and hope that made the principles work. They were taught to acknowledge the source of their strength. The sad truth is that they did not acknowledge that God was their source, and they did not teach their children the generational faithfulness of that God.

> *I will open my mouth in a parable: I will utter dark sayings of old: which we have heard and known, and our fathers have told us. We will not hide them from their children, showing to the generation to come the praises of the* LORD, *and his strength, and his wonderful works that he hath*

> *done. For he established a testimony in Jacob, and appointed a law in Israel, which he commanded our fathers, that they should make them known to their children: that the generation to come might know them, even the children which should be born; who should arise and declare them to their children: that they might set their hope in God, and not forget the works of God, but keep his commandments: and might not be as their fathers, a stubborn and rebellious generation; a generation that set not their heart aright, and whose spirit was not stedfast with God. The children of Ephraim, being armed, and carrying bows, turned back in the day of battle. They kept not the covenant of God, and refused to walk in his law; and forgat his works, and his wonders that he had showed them.* (Ps. 78:2–11)

The principle and pattern God reveals in Psalm 78 will work every time if it is followed. Parents are to teach their children, and their children will teach their children in the next generation. What do they teach? They are to teach *"the generation to come the praises of the Lord, and his strength, and his wonderful works that he hath done"* (Ps. 78:4). This helps their children to *"set their hope in God, and not forget the works of God"* (Ps. 78:7). Once our children forget God's faithfulness, they are in danger of committing the sin of the children of Ephraim. Although these men were well-prepared and armed, they turned back from the battle and from God's law and covenant.

Although God had done marvelous things in the sight of their fathers, evidently those fathers failed to successfully pass on to their children the strength and wonder of their God. As a result, the children of Ephraim:

1. *Fled* when faced with a challenge for which they were well prepared.
2. *Forgot* the actions of their fathers' covenant God. They lacked the keys to their success—already guaranteed by

the God of their forefathers. They turned and ran from what was legally theirs!

3. *Failed* or refused to walk in the law of their fathers' covenant God.

God intends for each succeeding generation to know more and more of His truth and of His law. He never intended for His people's children to go deeper and deeper into sin as Israel did. The generational principle set forth here is this: *Fathers are to obey God's law and to teach their children obedience to that law.*

One of the most basic and foundational needs in your children is their urgent need to understand the Lord God of their parents.

In Joshua 3, Joshua had led the people of Israel right up to the banks of the river Jordan. How were millions of people and their animals supposed to cross the swirling waters of the flood-swollen river? God told Joshua to send the priests carrying the Ark of the Covenant into the Jordan River first. As soon as their feet touched the water, the waters would separate and they would be able to cross the dry riverbed! They obeyed God and all the Israelites passed over. But God's work was not done.

At God's command, Joshua chose 12 men, one from each tribe of Israel. Then he told them to each take one stone out of the middle of the dry riverbed. The 12 stones were taken to a place where they were lodged and stacked. Why?

> *That this may be a sign among you, that when your children ask their fathers in time to come, saying, What mean ye by these stones?Then ye shall answer them, That the waters of Jordan were cut off before the ark of the covenant of the* L*ORD; when it passed over Jordan, the waters of Jordan were cut off: and these stones shall be for a memorial unto the children of Israel for ever.* (Josh. 4:6–7)

Family pictures, stories narrated, or diaries with recorded history can document the passage through difficult times and can testify of breakthroughs to succeeding generations. When Joshua had set up the stones in Gilgal, Joshua again commanded the fathers of his generation, *"When your children shall ask their fathers in time to come, saying, What mean these stones? Then ye shall let your children know...For the LORD your God dried up the waters of Jordan...that ye might fear the LORD your God for ever"* (Josh. 4:21-24).

God's Goal: That They Might Know Him as the Lord God

All parents should seek the Father's perspective concerning their role in His purposes. Our Father, the sovereign Lord and the Creator of all, cries out from the pages of history. His heart yearns for something He still has not found on the earth among all His created beings.

God's omnipotent greatness and the fullness of His being have set Him above His creatures. His love is more tender than that of a natural father, His mercy is more lavish than that of a doting mother, and His forgiveness and forgetfulness of our wrongdoing is more complete than that of the most forgetful father. Yet He still retains His ownership, His omniscience, His sovereign rulership, and His transcendence over all things.

God's great desire (for His being demands no less) is for your children to know Him as the Lord God. How you, as a parent, present God to your children will determine how the nations of men will perceive our Lord God in the next generation!

God has ordained that, as one holy nation, the church would honor Him as the Lord God. Then the hearts of men of all nations would both fear and know Him. Throughout His Word, God introduces a holy pattern that should transform the way we perceive the training of our children.

1. The eternal God wants to be known by all generations.
2. References to *Adonai, Jehovah,* Lord God, and The Self-Existent or Eternal One are found more than seven thousand times in the original Hebrew. Children begin to comprehend His eternal nature when they understand that He is the God of their forefathers.
3. God told Jacob, "[God Almighty shall] *give thee the blessing of Abraham, to thee, and to thy seed with thee; that thou mayest inherit the land wherein thou art a stranger, which God gave unto Abraham*" (Gen. 28:4).
4. God told Moses in Exodus 3:14–15: *"I AM THAT I AM...The LORD God of your fathers...this is my name for ever, and this is my memorial unto all generations."*
5. God affirmed His identity and history to unfaithful Israel in Hosea 12:9 and 13:4: "[I am] *the LORD thy God from the land of Egypt.*"
6. To the Hebrew children, God said, *"I am the LORD thy God, which have brought thee out of the land of Egypt, out of the house of bondage"* (Exod. 20:2).
7. God blessed the fathers' children in Deuteronomy 1:11: *"(The LORD God of your fathers make you a thousand times so many more as ye are, and bless you, as he hath promised you!)."*
8. God promised to fight for the fathers' children: *"The LORD your God which goeth before you, he shall fight for you, according to all that he did for you in Egypt before your eyes; and in the wilderness, where thou hast seen how that the LORD thy God bare thee, as a man doth bear his son, in all the way that ye went, until ye came into this place"* (Deut. 1:30–31).
9. God told the children to possess the land in Deuteronomy 4:1: *"Possess the land which the LORD God of your fathers giveth you."*

This divine pattern shows that the Lord our God wants us to know Him as a God of history, as a God who has historically blessed His people. The God of our fathers wants fathers to present Him to their children. In this way, He will truly be "I AM THAT I AM" or "I am the Lord who spans the generations." He made a covenant with our forefathers. He made a covenant with our fathers. Now, He wants to make a covenant with our children!

God's Transgenerational Blessings

In Exodus 2:23–25, the Bible says that God heard the cry of the Hebrews in their bondage and remembered the covenant He had made with their forefathers. There is a "generational rolling effect" of God's blessing revealed here. God blesses the fathers of one generation, and then blesses their children because He remembers the covenant promises He made with their fathers.

1. Fathers' blessings have a generational effect on their children.
2. Children inherit the blessings of their fathers to the extent that they acknowledge the Lord God of their fathers and walk in their fathers' godly ways.
3. Children can appeal to God on the basis of the covenant promises He made to their fathers and confirmed by His oath.

We Must Teach Our Children Right and Wrong

Many of our children face some serious problems today because of their lack of knowledge. God warned us, *"My people are destroyed for lack of knowledge"* (Hos. 4:6).

1. Our children do not know what's right!
2. Our children do not know what's wrong!
3. Our children do not know they don't "have a choice"!

These problems exist for exactly three reasons, although all three problems can be traced to one source.

1. Parents do not teach their children what is right.
2. Parents do not teach their children what is wrong.
3. Parents tell their children they "have a choice."

Again, there are three solutions, but every solution begins at the same "point source."

1. Parents, teach your children what is right.
2. Parents, teach your children what is wrong.
3. Parents, teach your children they don't "have a choice."

The Bible is our single most important source to help us teach our children right and wrong. God's Word contains all of the basic lessons on right and wrong, and it is very clear: Breaking His law means doing wrong.

For more than thirty years, there has been a methodically organized plot to eradicate the rule of God from the lives of men in modern society. The removal of God from the center of life and the placement of autonomous man on center stage has brought an appalling dependence on man as the source of truth. Another result has been a heightened trust in the decision-making power of man and in the power or importance of his "choice."

It is not uncommon to hear preachers present God's Word with His blessings that follow obedience and His sanctions against disobedience. However, after such a solid presentation of truth, they only follow it up with, "It's your choice." It is growing increasingly common to hear teachers present various cases with consequences attached, along with some grievous results of breaking some natural or supernatural law—then they end the class with the statement, "It's your choice."

Sadly, many parents do the same thing! After warning their children of impending sanctions and consequences when wrong decisions are made, parents often end with destructive statements like, "It's your choice," or "You're old enough," or "It's your decision!"

It is my observation and conclusion that these parents, leaders, and mentors fall into this trap because:

1. A large proportion of these preachers, teachers, and parents do not wish to accept responsibility for the actions of the children.
2. A large portion of these parents, teachers, and preachers actively and knowingly break the law (both natural and supernatural). Therefore, they do not feel they are in a position either to clearly state what's right or wrong or to demand godly obedience of children.
3. A large number of today's teachers and parents grew up under the influence of situational ethics and thus have matured into values-clarification weaklings. It is difficult for them to teach right and wrong because they were never taught the difference between right and wrong themselves. They have never discovered that God's Word boldly and authoritatively declares what is absolutely wrong and absolutely right. They cannot conceive of existence without wall-straddling, white lies, or gray areas. They simply do not know the difference between right and wrong and are therefore incompetent to teach the next generation!
4. A large proportion of parents "fear the faces" of their children. They honor their children above God and are unwilling to restrain them. Parents habitually take the convenient and easy way out by saying, "It's your choice!"
5. A growing number of fathers want to be considered "cool" by their children, and mothers who once solidly presented God's law and affirmed right or wrong now feel that since their children are 13, 16, 18, or 21 years of age, it's simply "their choice"! Quoting ages is often the parents' way of denying or rejecting their own sense of responsibility and their authority! God will one day make a judgment call on all of us who are parents and teachers. He will judge us by the extent to which we have taught our children God's law.

Either we will be blessed with a heritage of righteous seeds of promise as David was, or our lineage and inheritance, our anointing and promised generational blessing, will be cut off swiftly and sharply as Eli's were.

Eli the priest honored his sons above God. He chose not to restrain his sons and allowed them to flagrantly and repeatedly break God's laws. Eli died a tragic death and his sons were slain (1 Sam. 4:11, 17–18). His grandson and all of his posterity ultimately died out. His grandson was named Ichabod meaning *"the glory is departed from Israel"* (1 Sam. 4:21). What a shameful end for the line of a generation of priests who should have brought glory to their God and their nation!

My Son, Forgive Me: Some Reflections

For the many times I picked you up when you wanted to stand on your own,

For the many times I brought you gifts when all you needed was me,

For the doubts I held about you that made me withhold you from attempting tasks for which you were born,

And for the priceless little moments I crowded out with petty statements, while you groped for life-giving interchange,

I ask you to forgive me, my son.

How well do I remember your first birthday when you ran, not walked!

The day you wept as though your little heart would break at the world's injustice to the little ones.

And the spark, no, the little, red-hot flame of righteous anger I saw in your eyes,

And wondered…O God, this son…will he one day fight for the children?

The kindness that lights up your eyes whenever you hold a baby in your arms.

The warmth with which you wrap your little grandma in your arms, and your stout, swift determination to protect your brothers.

How much do I marvel at the way you grow taller and stronger, when others are held by you—a captive audience!

How closely do I watch your stride for that lift of confidence your eyes for that ray of kindness.

Your heart for that full love like no other.

For such a task were you created, my firstborn son,

To give life and love and kindness in your Father's name.

And nothing else will fill your heart

No expectations of the people. No comparison with your brothers

Nothing else will become gold in your hands until…

Until you do what you were born to do.

Speak boldly of injustice. Caress the hearts of your people with hope.

Fight for your brothers. Defend them from the rest…

And stand up for your firstborn rights.

Wrest them from the seed-devourer who seeks to dull the soul and spirit of natural-born deliverers.

For a child of destiny you are! A full-fledged child of destiny you are!

So this is a mother's declaraton for you, "Live, and not die!"

And may your followers be multitudes. And may your enemies lie

Wasted and vanquished at your feet! My child of destiny!

9
Raising Wise Winners

What is wisdom? And what is that gift of wisdom that makes a person stand superior to the rest? It is the gift of wisdom that makes the difference and gives the differential advantage to the wise leader. The critical advantages wise men have over foolish men provide the security, the well-being, and the resources that our children need. It is true to say that wisdom is the principal source of success for persons destined for success in national leadership.

Good parents eagerly hold on to God's promises for their children. The prophet Joel proclaimed a significant promise: *"I will pour out my spirit upon all flesh; and your sons and your daughters shall prophesy...your young men shall see visions: and upon the handmaids in those days will I pour out my spirit"* (Joel 2:28–29). We have taken this promise for ourselves. However, it's a promise of wisdom for our seed! The truth is that our children will outstrip us. They will be infused with a supernatural giftedness so that they will execute extraordinary feats. They will be endowed with abilities needed for national leadership.

What is the role and work of the Spirit in the lives of our children? The prophet Isaiah declared a similar blessing for our seed, demonstrating God's unchanging intention to raise up seed filled with wisdom: *"I will pour my spirit upon thy seed, and my blessing upon thine offspring"* (Isa. 44:3).

Even earlier than the prophecies of the prophets Joel and Isaiah, the cry of wisdom echoed God's desire and longing: *"Behold, I* [wisdom] *will pour out my spirit unto you, I will make known my words unto you"* (Prov. 1:23). The earliest existence of the spirit of wisdom is evidenced in the wonders of the created universe. The absolute perfection of the functioning of universal principles and laws declares the role of wisdom.

Wisdom is God's provision for the extension of life to the young. It is the creative force of God, existing with Him before and during creation, yet still sustaining life.

The cry of wisdom reveals a truth that is crucial to the fulfillment of purpose in our children of promise. It is wisdom personified in Christ that cries out, "I will pour out My Spirit unto you." The entire book of Proverbs contains hundreds of practical teachings that will bring life to every young person who will follow their lead. On the other hand, if they neglect to walk in wisdom, then poverty, illness, and subsequently death become the sure result. Wisdom, like the heart of our Father God, cries out for all to run to receive the blessing of the Spirit who brings life.

Proverbs 8 describes the "activity" of wisdom in the beginning, before the earth was made. Wisdom was always *with* God, *possessed* by God, and was the daily *delight* of God. Wisdom appears to be God's life-giving energy. *"For by me thy days shall be multiplied"* (Prov. 9:11). Wisdom is the craftsman, the supreme intelligence behind all physical and metaphysical laws and principles.

Wisdom Begins with the Decision to Obey Godly Instruction

It is a life of wisdom that will preserve the lives of our sons and daughters! Wisdom stands at the top of the high places and cries, *"Unto you, O men, I call; and my voice is to the sons of man"* (Prov. 8:4). Wisdom makes its appeal to the same sons and daughters who are targeted by a ruthless adversary who seeks to destroy them.

The opposite of a wise man is a fool. The apostle Paul described a fool by recounting the depths of sexual perversity and lawlessness of the unredeemed man. *"Professing themselves to be wise, they became fools....Who knowing the judgment of God, that they which commit such things are worthy of death, not only do the same, but have pleasure in them that do them"* (Rom. 1:22, 32). Paul literally defined "foolishness" as knowing God's judgment (consequences) and still reveling in disobedience. Therefore, wisdom is the decision to obey God's law and the standards of right living. It is not only the determination to do right but also the absence of pleasure in the companionship of those who persist in doing wrong or in foolish action.

Paul also wrote, *"Let the word of Christ dwell in you richly in all wisdom...And whatsoever ye do in word or deed, do all in the name of the Lord Jesus"* (Col. 3:16–17). Wisdom is doing. It is the activity of "walking out" good deeds toward God, others, and one's self. It is the power or energy to do right.

Wisdom is the practical application of knowledge and understanding. It begins with a decision to do the wise things, which leads to life instead of loss and death. Wisdom always warns the young to remember the certain consequences of choices and actions. Proverbs 7 gives a classic example of the meaning of wisdom. *Wisdom is making the right decisions based on knowledge and understanding of consequences.*

These consequences will be either blessings or curses. In Proverbs 7, a young man is warned by Wisdom not to go the way of the careless young man who is seduced by a wayside prostitute. Wisdom warns that the woman will subtly lure her victim to a perfumed bed with fake promises of offerings and love. The foolish youth who goes after her is *"as an ox* [that] *goeth to the slaughter…till a dart strike through his liver....*[He] *knoweth not that it is for his life....Her house is the way to hell, going down to the chambers of death"* (Prov. 7:22–23, 27). We must diligently warn our own children to remember the warnings in God's Word and urge them to choose the way of wisdom.

Who Are Wise Children?

1. Wise children know their Father God as their sovereign Lord.
2. Wise children know that God is a holy God who is just and gracious and who gives blessings for obedience. They also realize that disobedience brings just punishment.
3. Wise children fear God and choose to obey God rather than man.
4. Wise children know God's Word and remember it.
5. Wise children make decisions based on what God says. They remember God's Word and they want to please God through loving obedience.
6. Wise children are continually directed by God's divine energy (wisdom) at work within them. It is a rich creative energy that brings rich rewards.
7. Wise children become empowered by the life and creativity of wisdom and become God's instruments to bring His order, harmony, blessing, and kingdom on the earth!

Wisdom brings long life, health, wealth, strength to stand up to temptation, truth in one's understanding and words, obedience to parents, love of learning, diligence, a benevolent spirit, and self-control.

Wisdom is knowing God's Word, believing that Word, and living by that Word. If our children have God's Word always at work in their hearts and spirits, they will walk in wisdom, please God, and not lead lives of sin. Wisdom will give them constant ability to do what brings God's blessing.

The opposite of wisdom is foolishness. The foolish child brings heaviness to his parents (Prov. 10:1) and dishonor to God. The book of Proverbs describes the traits and choices that characterize foolish children.

To be "foolish" means to still be in need of correction, training, and shaping. To be foolish is to disregard God's Word and warnings, even though they warn us that we are taking a downward path to destruction.

1. A foolish child is easily enticed or fooled (Prov. 7:7), but he is not open to your teaching.
2. A foolish child is stubborn and refuses to change, but he will repeat his foolish actions (Prov. 26:11).
3. A foolish child does not accept correction or reproof. In fact, he hates correction or instruction (Prov. 9:7–8; 18:2).
4. A foolish child later mocks at wrongdoing (Prov. 14:9).
5. A foolish child is proud and haughty (Prov. 16:18).
6. A foolish child turns his back on wisdom (Prov. 9:7–8).
7. A foolish child says, *"There is no God,"* and, in his attitude, acts as if God does not exist (Ps. 14:1).
8. A foolish child does not care about the needs of the hungry and thirsty (Prov. 22:6, 9).
9. A foolish child is talkative and does not think before be speaks (Prov. 10:8, 19).
10. A foolish child does not fear the Lord (Prov. 1:29). He does not have a relationship with God who rules the affairs

of men, who has laws, and who blesses obedience and curses disobedience.

Passing the Test of Wisdom and Prudence

Just as the seasons of seedtime and harvest come and go, all parents know the day will come when their children will have to stand on their own as self-sufficient adults. That simply means they must stand or fall according to their own choices and decisions.

This is the trepidation of every parent's heart (unless, as Proverbs 22:6 says, the child was raised up *"in the way he should go,"* from God's Word). When a child reaches his eighteenth birthday or leaves home for college, the questions and the fears come again and again to the parents. "Will my child make godly and wise decisions? Is my child breaking God's law in the secret times and places? Is my child snared by the fear of man? Will my seed go the way of the young man who was seduced in Proverbs 7 and whose punishment was death?"

The only guarantee a parent can have that a child will make godly decisions is if that child is wise. If you have raised your child to be wise, then your child will make decisions based on a knowledge of God's Word and a rich memory of consequences. The wise child will choose to do things God's way. He will not be easily enticed, nor will he steal, lie, or waste his talents or resources. He will refuse to be the companion of idle fools.

Acting with Wisdom Depends on Covenant Relationship

The first priority for our children should be to develop a covenant relationship with God. Our children must be taught over and over what God's Word says. They should have a covenant relationship with a holy God who loves man and has set laws, ordinances, and restrictions in place so that we can live pure, holy, and full lives.

It is from this relationship with God that a deep desire will arise in our children to please their Father and walk in a close fellowship of obedience to Him. This releases the dynamic energy for righteous action, so powerfully at work in the Godhead, to flow through the Holy Spirit to our children. It is through this relationship that wisdom is released to teach and empower the children of God.

Wise children will develop loving, respectful relationships with family members and others. It is within these covenant relationships that they learn to love fully, think generously, and give and receive gracefully. These lifelong covenants should be guarded and not broken, so that our wise children will learn to walk in wisdom, contributing their life skills and godly gifts to society.

Every aspect of your children's lives—their relationship to God and to others, their care of their own bodies and their treatment of others, the use of their tongues and their level of well-being—are all related to their level of wisdom. The following are three examples.

	God's Word	Wisdom Characteristic
1.	Proverbs 22:20–21	Your children will speak words of truth and not tell lies.

Have not I written to thee excellent things in counsels and knowledge, that I might make thee know the certainty of the words of truth; that thou mightest answer the words of truth to them that send unto thee?

2	Proverbs 2:9–10	Your child will enjoy hearing and studying.

Then shalt thou understand righteousness, and judgment, and equity; yea, every good path. When wisdom entereth into thine heart, and knowledge is pleasant unto thy soul.

3. Proverbs 13:20 — Your children's best friends pursue wisdom, knowledge, and understanding. They do not have fools as their companions.

He that walketh with wise men shall be wise: but a companion of fools shall be destroyed.

Your children's success in life, in their relationships with God, and with other wise persons will depend on the extent to which they:

1. Have learned to honor and fear God.
2. Are trained in the Word of God.
3. Are trained to choose God's way.
4. Are restrained from doing foolishness.
5. Remember God's warnings about obedience.
6. Walk in wisdom or make right, godly decisions.
7. Remember God's words of promise and blessing resulting from wise actions.

The Wisdom Quotient: WQ or IQ?

One conventional standard of testing currently used to evaluate children is the intelligence test. Various intelligence tests supposedly measure a child's verbal and nonverbal ability as well as psychomotor speed, range of knowledge, and other competencies. Once a child's performance is measured, he is placed in a category with other children of similar rank.

Scores or intelligence quotients are based on a comparison of the subject's performance with the performance of others in a standardized sample. This intelligence quotient (IQ) often becomes a label that can powerfully affect a child's school placement, educational program, and how others perceive him.

However, although the IQ may be associated with a child's learning potential and academic achievement, it does not convey a true picture of the "whole man." Although a high IQ may bring a person a top managerial position, it does not guarantee success. A high IQ rating does not guarantee good relationships with God or with other people. It does not produce self-confidence, riches, good health, or honor. Only a high "wisdom quotient" (WQ) guarantees a good life and the blessings and favor of God and man.

Appendix D contains the Morgan Wisdom Scale, a screening instrument designed to help parents determine their child's status and growth in wisdom. It contains a cross section of wisdom indicators taken from the book of Proverbs.

Each of the twenty-five items represents a "domain" of wisdom. A domain is a discrete field of behaviors that reflects your child's functioning in that area. For example, item 18 measures a child's performance in obedience to parents' instruction. Each item covers an area where wisdom brings high scores as well as godly blessing and rewards, or where foolishness brings low scores. Low scores reflect a child's current functioning and predisposition to disobedience, dishonor, and spiritual retardation.

Let me warn you, though, that the Morgan Wisdom Scale is only a screening device. It attempts to measure your child's current functioning or predisposition. It should not be used to label or categorize a child or to imply an inability to change.

How to Use the Results of the WQ

The total score of the Morgan Wisdom Scale gives parents a measure of their child's current functioning in wisdom. High scores may reflect the following:

1. The level or extent to which parents and teachers have taught wisdom to the child.

2. A child's willingness to benefit from teachings based on godly biblical principles provided by parents and significant adults.
3. A child's current functioning in his present circumstances (family, social).
4. The availability of godly teachers.
5. The manner in which parents have reared, taught, and trained the child. (For example, was the child raised with permissiveness, overindulgence, harsh punitive authoritarianism, or with patient, persistent, loving guidance?)
6. A child's age or social maturity.

A high score indicates adequate or superior spiritual growth in wisdom. A low score may indicate a child's urgent need for help or simply a lack of opportunity for growth in an area. Parents should identify areas of weakness and offer opportunities for growth to strengthen them.

Your Child Needs Help

When a child's WQ pinpoints a problem, the first step parents and teachers should take is to identify the specific areas where the child has a failing or low score. Steps should be taken to make adequate arrangements to strengthen the child's spiritual growth in wisdom. The character traits covered by the Wisdom Scale include honesty, chastity, obedience, love of study, and fear of the Lord.

Second, each item with a failing score should be looked at separately, and then a specific program should be designed to help the child in that area. For instance, if the child persistently tells lies, then it is important to teach that child the value of truth. In this particular case, the following ideas may be useful:

1. Appeal to the child on the basis of his relationship with God. "God loves you; He does not want you to break His law. He is displeased when you do." Your approach should *not* be, "I told you not to tell lies!" but rather "God's Word says."
2. Identify the source of the deceit, point it out, and identify relevant Scripture references that should be taught.
3. Insist on truth. No white lies are allowed. Don't accept your child's affirmation of lies. He should not get used to speaking in half-truths or being comfortable with speaking lies.

How Often Should the "WQ" Be Measured?

Once every nine to twelve months should be an adequate frequency for measuring the WQ. The Wisdom Scale is most effective when it is re-administered to measure progress achieved after additional teaching and training in wisdom has been received.

How to Administer the Morgan Wisdom Scale

1. You will need a copy of the scale and a pencil.
2. This scale may be completed by an older child on his own. If the subject is a younger child, it should be done by a parent who knows the child very well.
3. Read the first page, which contains a short paragraph on wisdom and directions for completion.
4. If the child is doing it on his own, say: "This is a scale to tell you about how you perform in many different areas. It is not a test. Look at the first page. First read the short passage on wisdom then read the instructions at the bottom of the page."
5. "Complete the first page. Turn to the second page. For each item, first read the Scripture key or the Scripture verses.

Then read the statement. Then score yourself out of 5. Your score should reflect the extent to which the statement is true for you. The higher the score, the more the statement is true. Be thorough. Do not leave any blank.

"Total your scores for the 25 items. Turn to the last page and use the formula to complete your wisdom quotient (WQ). Then identify your present level of functioning and your growth in wisdom." This scale may be completed by a parent, using the directions just given. The scale may also be administered simultaneously to a group of children of similar age by an adult.

How to Teach Your Children to Hear God's Voice

One of the most important keys to raising children of promise is to teach them how to hear the voice of the Lord their God. Young Samuel heard God's voice and led his generation back to godliness. Remember, hearing God's voice must be preceded by knowing or recognizing God's voice. This in turn will only take place if a child develops a relationship with God. If your child knows God, then he will recognize His voice. Whenever and however He speaks, he will know it. That inner voice will remind your children of values and principles, rules and laws, warnings and consequences. Let's teach our children to recognize that voice and to obey what God says.

The Major Tasks of the Parent

1. Parents' primary task is to ensure their children's relationships with God. As we communicate with God ourselves, acknowledge His presence in our homes, and submit ourselves and all family matters to God, our children will naturally move toward an abiding and acute awareness of God.
2. Another task of parents is to "demystify" the idea of "hearing God's voice." Many books and opinions have

been written on what is perceived as a mystery—that of hearing God's voice. Is it a thunderous noise? A still small voice? The questions continue. The truth is that:

a. God is always speaking to our hearts and minds.

b. God desires to be heard.

c. God has committed Himself to speaking to us, whether it be through impressions, thoughts, direct visitations, or with an audible voice. Proverbs 1:23 says, *"I will make known my words unto you."*

3. As parents routinely hear God speaking and as they acknowledge His voice, their children will know that this is a normal occurrence. As parents hear and discern, their children will also know God's voice.
4. Parents should be always willing to defer to God's voice. It is tempting for parents to say, "Son, I want you to do this..." or "Daughter, I believe you should go this way...." Instead, parents should acknowledge that it was the voice of God that the child heard and God's wisdom that he or she acquired. They should say, "Children, God has said you should...." No wonder children do not know that God speaks to us! We prefer to get the glory of leadership ourselves! Remember, it is more important for your child to hear God's voice than yours!
5. Hearing God's voice means obeying what God says. Joshua 24:24 says, *"The LORD our God will we serve, and his voice will we obey."* To hear is to do. Parents must cultivate a spirit of obedience, for it is not enough to hear God's voice. Joshua placed a stone in their midst and said, *"Behold, this stone shall be a witness unto us; for it hath heard all the words of the LORD which he spake unto us"* (verse 27). All created things hear God's words, but your child was created to hear and to obey. Obedience depends not so much on whether a child hears God's voice, but on the degree of the child's submission and love for God.

6. Teach your children to read God's Word with the understanding that "this is what the Lord is saying." Give life to the written Word. Act upon it. Your child will learn that to hear God's voice is to obey.
7. Teach your sons and daughters to desire communion with their Father. As it was natural for Adam and Eve to desire communion with God and He with them, so too God waits to see your children desire His fellowship. Actively promote this relationship. Say, "Now, after you have finished your meal, go to your quiet place and talk to your Father God. He is waiting!" Then afterward, ask your child, "What did you say to God?" and "What did God say to you?" I guarantee you that God will always speak and that your child will know what He said. As your child reports to you, his confession will strengthen his knowledge that God speaks and that he can hear His voice!
8. Cultivate within your child a spirit that yearns for a quiet place, a spirit that loves silence and meditation. Your house should provide those comfortable private corners that can become places where your child can meet with his Father God. It is order and harmony, not chaos, that enhances your child's readiness to relate with God. Within that atmosphere of serenity, peace, and quiet anticipation, your child will learn to communicate and have dialogue with the God of his fathers.
9. Encourage your child to go to God with his questions or with his everyday "chatter" about commonplace events. "Go to your room and ask God about..." should be one of your usual statements. Your child will learn to depend on God for his decision making. Nehemiah the prophet wrote, *"Then I consulted with myself, and I rebuked the nobles"* (Neh. 5:7). Nehemiah had discovered his inner store of wisdom and counsel in the quiet place with God. He was therefore able to trust himself. This trust was built on

his relationship and knowledge of his Father's voice, His works, and His ways.

Teach Your Children How to Laugh and Play

A wise leader knows how to laugh and play. Children live what they learn. Do you laugh? Do you play? Your children will imitate what they see in your own behavior.

For years, the physical education programs of many schools have highlighted the importance of exercise in retaining physical and mental health. Programs have also tended to stress the value of physical development for personal well-being and interpersonal dynamic growth, team spirit, and intra-group competition.

The one thing that is sadly lacking in such programs is the need for sports for their own sake, for enjoyment, for pleasure, and for recreation. Have your children learned to play? Are they able to enjoy a game whether they win or lose?

School physical fitness programs do not generally list as an objective "the basic need of your child to laugh." The Bible says, *"To every thing there is a season, and a time to every purpose under the heaven:...a time to laugh"* (Eccl. 3:1, 4). And there's a time to weep! It also says, *"A merry heart doeth good like a medicine"* (Prov. 17:22).

Another phenomenon that has developed over the past twenty years is the transformation of the once friendly, competitive neighborhood games. Now we can watch fathers yell at their children, curse the coaches, and engage in fistfights with other fathers at their children's baseball games. Now the children play to make their dads look good, to walk in their fathers' footsteps (the old "when I was your age" syndrome), and to become what their fathers never became in college and adulthood. As parents, we need to reassess our hidden and ulterior motives.

Many children never really learn to play! Very few children are taught to feel that sense of vigorous participation and anticipation of triumph; that determination to fight for victory regardless of personal sacrifice. Many lack a sense of reckless abandon to play for its own sake. To lose and laugh, to congratulate the other, to possess a total dominance over that ball and over one's own weakness, and to climb above and beyond it in total and full laughter is truly rewarding.

In this atmosphere, the enjoyment of winning is just as important as having a good game and losing. This is where a child's ringing peaks of laughter, spontaneous moans of disappointment, and even tearful acceptance of defeat together make up a love of play for its own sake.

How Can Parents Help Their Young Children Play?

1. Watch your own reaction or response. An appropriate response is the best. A response becomes inappropriate when disappointment quickly turns to anger, or when commendation gives way to scathing remarks about doing better next time.
2. Give open, full, and lavish praise where that is due. It's a myth that says too much praise leads to "swollen heads"!
3. Celebrate victory! Have a party! Laugh about the great plays and the great mistakes too! Your relationship with your child is more important than his infallibility on the baseball field!
4. Often recall and recount good times together and seek opportunities to highlight the joys.
5. Engage in a variety of activities that bring pleasure to family members.
6. Plan special vacation experiences around activities that bring joy and laughter to all family members. Make

allowance for each other, for the youngest and the oldest, and for the extrovert and the introvert also!

7. Let your homes ring out with happy sounds—good music, loud game playing, quiet laughter, and the merry hum of pleasurable activity. Invest in needed materials—exciting family games, a table tennis set, and good books. Play with your children.
8. Have family concerts and encourage creativity and generous family commendation.
9. Meal times should be times of leisurely, conversational sharing. Use the after-dinner times for storytelling with dad, passing down old family tales from one generation to another.
10. And remember—it's all right to laugh! Our spirits were made to play and to enjoy the fullness of fellowshipping with each other and with the Father. Your children's first impulse is to laugh! They will laugh their way into political office, into the mayoral office, and among the oppressed, whom they will make rejoice!

A wise child with a love for his nation and for his people grows up to be a wise leader and a person of substance and of stature. Our seed of destiny will change their environment and affect their generation for good.

10
Prophesy to Your Seed

How Does God Bind Us to Hope for Our Nations?

Where does hope for our nations lie? In our children! Are you willing to share your children with your nation? Are you prepared to bring forth the hope for your nation out of your seed? God is looking for men and women whose lives will be inextricably bound to their nation. God sovereignly causes godly men and women to bring forth children. As these children are raised within a nation, they will be affected by events in the life of that nation, but they themselves can, and will, bring change in that nation!

It is God's *modus operandi* to bind a man to his nation by giving him children. Loving parents are not willing to see their seed cast adrift in a failing nation that would consume their seed in its own death struggle. Godly parents who are able to perceive the times and the seasons will fight and work to organize and preserve the life of their nation. Parents who work to preserve their nation preserve their children as well, for the nation is the "seedbed" for the prosperity and growth of their seed. As godly parents organize and strategize for the benefit of their God-given seed, their nation will receive the overflow of that benefit.

For many, the idea that God actually deals with and concerns Himself with nations is new and hard to receive. The fact is that God created the social order of man with its subdivisions of races, nations, language groups, and authority structures. The history of nations is marked by good leaders liberating nations and moving toward a better life for the people. Throughout the Bible, God's dealings with entire nations stand out as an enduring pattern.

God isn't satisfied to simply see one or two families redeemed from a nation. He wants the whole nation. Again and again, God has acted to save an entire nation of people. He actively raises up saviors from among His people to deliver nations. God's word to you and me is simple and direct. "Your children are My seed. They were born to declare My glory to the generations. As My nation-builders, and as chosen stewards over My heritage, I charge you to raise up your seed to lead their nation to Me."

Would You Father a Nation?

From the beginning in the Garden of Eden, God has sought seed. First, He created an entire race in His own image and likeness. He gave them a free will so they could offer worship and companionship as sons and daughters without compulsion or fear. Adam and Eve chose to sin, and their seed—the entire race of man—was separated from their destiny. The knowledge of God began to fade from the generations of man, so God sought one man, Noah, to carry on His purposes.

After the great Flood, the process of raising up a race and a single nation of sons and daughters unto God began anew. Once again, wrong choices and the indelible sin nature in man's heart led to a misuse of unity, and man was then separated by God into nations. As the race deteriorated from generation to generation into heathenish and pagan practices and a flagrant lack of rule, the knowledge of God seemingly disappeared from the race of man.

God once again revealed yet another masterstroke: He sought out and separated to Himself one man who responded to his Creator. This one man of simple faith would be the father of a nation. Abraham also would not only make a covenant with God, but he also would commit himself to be separate and apart from his brethren and from the ungodly nations. He undertook all measures, including circumcision, to separate his seed unto God. God's purpose was to raise up a holy nation that would, in turn, draw the other nations back into God's family.

The strident call is for a group of good men and women with the stamp of destiny and wisdom to raise up seed of destiny. They would undertake all measures to assume leadership roles and to shape their nations.

God Calls for Children to Be Born

When God decides to raise up a nation, He calls for children to be born! He did it in the case of David, the king of Israel. He caused Jeremiah to be conceived when Israel badly needed a prophet, and he caused a previously barren Hannah to conceive a child who was to replace a family of disobedient priests. God sees the need in the nations where prophets, kings, and priests lose their anointing. Then he creates a child in the womb of a woman. Moses is a prime example of a liberator who was born during the bitterest time of slavery and oppression in Israel.

God calls for man to transgenerationally pass on to his children the covenant promise of God. God operates on the earth through our seed. Our seed must be willing to be the fathers and mothers of nations. The history of our children will determine the history of our nation. The fulfillment of God's promises to Abraham was directly dependent upon the extent to which he taught his children and the extent to which his children obeyed him (Gen. 18:17–19).

Prophecy Unfolds from the Womb

Very few fathers will choose to willingly "walk in the shoes" of the prophet Isaiah. This man had a high calling of God on his life. Why did God demand this much from a man? Upon what kind of man does God make this type of demand?

The ministry of Isaiah the prophet spanned across the reign of several kings. Although Judah and Israel flourished as one nation under David and Solomon, the nation later turned away from God and became a *"sinful nation, a people laden with iniquity, a seed of evildoers, children that are corrupters"* (Isa. 1:4). The nation split into two parts, Israel and Judah, during Isaiah's time. The prophet called heaven and earth to witness the sadness of God at His children's rebellion. God was about to bring judgment on Israel.

Once again, God refused to simply tell His chosen seed, "It's your choice." Although the people knew that their choice was involved, they didn't realize how determined their Father was to redeem them—and every other nation through them.

God called Isaiah to be more than just a voice to his nation (Isa. 6); He also made another major demand of Isaiah. In Isaiah 8:1–4, God told Isaiah to call witnesses to record His prophetic word to the prophet, as well as its literal and prophetic fulfillment. These witnesses, Uriah and Zechariah, recorded God's prophecy concerning Isaiah and his wife, who was a prophetess. When these parents came together, a son was conceived who was to be named *Maher-shalal-hash-baz,* which literally means "haste the plunder, haste the spoil." God explained that this son of Isaiah the prophet was to bear this name because before the child would be able to speak clearly, Damascus and Samaria (symbolic of Israel and Judah) would be spoiled by the enemy king of Assyria. The prophecy was literally fulfilled twenty-one months later—when Isaiah's son was twelve months old!

Step into the Prophet's Shoes

The events described in the book of Isaiah literally happened; they are not merely nice stories with a message. Step into Isaiah's shoes to get a sense of the power of God's acts on behalf of a nation.

Your nation is in trouble because of its sin. In fact, God's hand of judgment is raised over your nation and He has called you to preach judgment. Things have not gone well. The people are still unrepentant, and you are stuck with living in the middle of the mess. Now the determined and unpredictable God you serve begins to speak to you again: "I want you to have a son—now! I want you to call him, 'haste the plunder, haste the spoil.' Before he can say, 'Daddy,' your nation will be overrun."

What God was actually saying was this: "Yes, I want you to bring up a son in this nation. In this way, I will make you feel the pain of the nation. You will fight for its preservation. You will give your life for the preservation of your son. And thus your nation stands a chance for survival!" (Now how do you feel about walking in Isaiah's shoes?)

Hosea: A True Prophetic Father

Hosea the prophet was another man who was called into "prophetic fatherhood" by God to save his nation. Israel was "prostituting" itself with the other nations. *"There is no truth, nor mercy, nor knowledge of God in the land....My people are destroyed for lack of knowledge"* (Hos. 4:1, 6). God brought a judgment against the nation: *"because thou hast rejected knowledge, I will also reject thee, that thou shalt be no priest to me: seeing thou hast forgotten the law of thy God, I will also forget thy children"* (Hos. 4:6).

God's Masterstroke

Against this setting of sin, rejection, and idolatry, God the Father revealed yet another masterstroke of strategy and love to redeem His betrothed nation of priests.

1. God told Hosea to take a wife from one of the idolatrous nations prostituting his land. He was saying, "You will understand how I feel to have Israel for a wife."
2. Then God told Hosea he would have a son, and He told him to call his son, *Jezreel,* which means "scattered." God promised, *"for yet a little while, and I will avenge the blood of Jezreel upon the house of Jehu, and will cause to cease the kingdom of the house of Israel....I will break the bow of Israel in the valley of Jezreel"* (Hos. 1:4–5). The prophet Hosea clearly prophesied that Israel would be scattered into all the lands.
3. Then Hosea and his wife had a daughter and named her *Loruhamah,* meaning "unpitied": *"For I will no more have mercy upon the house of Israel"* (Hos. 1:6).
4. Hosea's wife, Gomer, had another son. They were told, *"Call his name* ***Loammi*** [meaning 'not my people']*: for ye are not my people, and I will not be your God"* (Hos. 1:9).

Hosea and Gomer were called by God and given precious seed in whose very names were revealed the history of their people. They shared the fate of their people although they were innocent, and now they will forever be a symbol of God's judgment of a people.

The call of a man becomes a call of repentance to a nation. God's judgment on a nation becomes a judgment on children. *"Seeing thou hast forgotten the law of thy God, I will also forget thy children"* (Hos. 4:6).

A land or nation comes under God's judgment when He finds no mercy, no truth, and no knowledge in it. When He sees perversion and idolatry of every kind, He will demand the ministry of priests, prophets, and kings. In Hosea's case, God ensured a prophet's commitment to his call by linking him by his children to his nation and its blessings or judgment.

Jesus: Savior of the World

The Setting

God the Father created the world and man; man fell into sin and deserved the punishment of death. God gave a promise in Genesis 3:15 that the seed of a woman would conquer Satan. Although man had become desperately wicked (Gen. 6:5–7), God the Father placed His divine hope for the salvation of the world in His first and only begotten Son. The seed of the Deliverer, from generation to generation, is preserved by God the Father who invests in the seed of Adam and Eve.

God's Gift

God called Mary and Joseph, who were betrothed to be married and who hoped, no doubt, to have a "normal" family. Mary, still unmarried and a virgin, was told by an angel that she would have a son who would save the world and that He should be called Jesus (which means "Savior").

Mary and Joseph were given the tremendous responsibility of bringing up a son whose very name said that He was born to die. He was to be trained for His purpose: to face death in complete obedience to the will of His heavenly Father. His heavenly Father took His best, His beloved, and His only Son, sent Him in the likeness of sinful flesh, and then gave Him for a world of nations. *"For God so loved the world, that he gave his only begotten Son"* (John 3:16).

Just as God loved the world, so Joseph and Mary were to gain a love for their people. They had to be willing for their son's life to be given for their nation and for the entire world. As God *"spared not his own Son"* (Rom. 8:32) so too the parents of Jesus had to completely detach themselves from "the Father's business" that Jesus had come to execute, and fully give Jesus over to God's plan for His life. His earthly parents always had to remember that Jesus was God's Son. This constant awareness transposed Joseph and Mary into another dimension, the dimension of divine alignment, where their own wills were in alignment with the will of God the Father.

As these young parents in a turbulent age watched the sinfulness of the generation increase, they also watched their son grow. But this Son was the hope of Israel; destiny pervaded His every word and deed. So these parents pondered these things in their hearts and raised Jesus to be fully conscious of His purpose. Jesus not only knew every prophetic word spoken of Him, but He also actively brought these prophecies to pass. Concerning His betrayal and death, Jesus said, *"But how then shall the scriptures be fulfilled, that thus it must be?...But all this was done, that the scriptures of the prophets might be fulfilled"* (Matt. 26:54, 56).

What of Father God Himself?

God the Father is our supreme prototype of every earthly parent to seeds of purpose and promise. Consider the following presuppositions:

In order to save the world He created and so loved, God had to bring something out of Himself...

1. To which He was inextricably tied.
2. Which pushed Him from eternity into the dimension of time.
3. Which bound Him to the future.

4. Who (the Person of Jesus) had to be a part of God coming out of His covenant Trinity relationship.
5. Who had to be obedient to Him.
6. Who had to be a Son of purpose.
7. Who had to be raised in such a way that He would know His roots (in God), know His purpose (as spoken by the prophets), and actively pursue that purpose *"that the scriptures of the prophets might be fulfilled."*

Isaiah and Hosea are two examples of parents who were called to walk in the footsteps of the Father. God said, "You will bear children. You will watch them grow up in your nation. You will warn your nation of My judgment. The life of your child depends upon it."

God Works through Generations

God's children, His works, and His purposes are inextricably tied together. God's operation in time is through children and generations. This is what the Lord is saying:

Your sons shall be My measuring stick for you and your nation.

I shall measure you by the life of your sons.

Your sons shall be My means of processing you.

Your sons' purpose will be to measure the times, as My measuring stick for judgment of their generation.

I shall cause sons to be born so that I can prolong your days, so that I can extend My Word, My judgment, and My mercy on a generation!

A son shall be My means of processing My purposes, of plumbing the depth of a people's response to My Word.

I relate with the world as a Father does, and so, I am tied to the world by the need I have for My sons to fulfill the purpose I have given them.

A prophet to a nation must be inextricably tied to that nation. He must father sons whose history and future destiny are bound up in that nation.

As a father speaks forth the prophetic intention of God for his son, so will he speak forth a prophetic word for his nation.

You will never father a nation unless you are yourself bound to the hope for the future life and prosperity of that nation.

For I shall cause you to love the sons of this nation, so you will burn with a passion for their survival and their salvation.

Their blood that runs on your streets is your blood—for you too must father your children within your nation.

When I look upon your people, I see sons, sons, sons...all born to preserve the old and bring in the new...all made to be the measuring stick, the plumb line for their nation.

Raise your sons...

as if your life depended on it.

as if their lives depended on it.

as if your nation's life depended on it.

The following is the cry of this mother's heart and the revelation I received from God as I argued with Him concerning my daughter and her call. She had recently made the decision to work among the needy and also accepted the invitation to work at a large crusade in the city of Kingston. I was quite pleased when I thought that that meant that she would perhaps be singing in the choir! However she informed us that she had consented to work in the deliverance tent. That meant she would be doing work among persons believed to be demon-possessed! That was not what this parent had in mind! The result was a series of questions to God and His gentle revelation of His purpose for "Sons of the Soil."

Sons of the Soil

Sons of the soil…

This native land of ours still obeys Your divine decree, Creator God, to bring forth sons.

And You, our own Father God, still breathe into these sons of the soil Your father life and Spirit.

And still You birth Your image life in these, our sons.

So securely are they tied to the earthly umbilical cord of their native land

And as securely bonded to the spirit breath of their natural Father God!

This land and God the Creator have both fathered my sons:

The one yielding its dust, and the other His Spirit breath

And thus His life and likeness.

But these sons of the soil, whose are they?

Yours, Creator God? Or mine?

The land that gave them birth, and by divine decree offers up its herbs and plants for food,

Still offers them its warmth and sunshine,

And beckons them with its joyous laughter and its carefree songs.

And all their hopes and their dreams are wrapped up in the heart of their sweet Jamaica-land!

To its own sons, my own sons seem so bonded!

And how their deepest passions awake to the cries of their people,

And how naturally they dance to the rhythm of their people's songs!

And yes! How they weep with those who mourn and sing the songs of the free warrior with those who yearn for freedom.

When I carried each in my own receiving earthly womb,

When my own lifeblood was spilt at the birth of my seed and fell upon this land,

When I "buried their navel strings" in this warm receiving womb of this land, and

When the blood of their circumcision was hurled to the hungry earth

Like Zipporah, I wondered if my husband too, like Moses of old was a "bloody husband" to me.

Was this land and its Yahweh God also demanding the life of my sons as well?

Did all that blood sink deep into the dust and become one with it?

Did that act bind my sons

And link the forever to the father-land?

And to the land of the Father God?

Does that blood still cry out to its God and claim its space and demand its earthly share of property and of land?

Does that blood still comingle and intermix with the blood of its brothers,

And all the sons of all its women-mothers, and

All the circumcision covenants of its men-fathers?

Creator Father God, is this Your way? Your divine transmission of Your life into a nation's life?

Through the lifeblood of my sons?

My sons, whose are they? Mine? Or Yours?

This lifeblood link with You, and

This lifeblood link with the land,

Does it guarantee the continued eternal outworking of Your "Let Us make man"?

It is only because I have a woman's heart that I can dare to understand it all. For understand I must! For I, too, have learnt from my Creator God the generous act of birthing and birthing and birthing again!

And I, too, must survive and recreate my life in sons, and

The faith of my sons must live,

And that of my sons' sons, too!

And they shall have their rightful share of land and property

And they shall solidly defend their land.

Like You, God of Ezekiel of old, they will say, as You did when You looked upon the prostitution of the land You loved so well

In the day when, full of sin, she lay open to the scorn, adultery, and reproach of other nations

And when I passed by thee

And saw thee wallowing in thine own blood

I said unto thee

When thou wast in thy blood, "Live!"

Yea, I said unto thee when thou wast in thy blood, "Live!"

Even so, shall this land of mine live one day because this day I freely give to You my sons!

And though sometimes I feel my heart would break

And I would look in anger at the lostness of my people,

the weakness of its fathers,

the tiredness of its mothers

And I would want to flee to a "better land,"

Yet the blood of my sons calls me, too, back to my land, the empty, cheerless eyes of your sons draw me to my land, into their depths,

And I, too, am caught up in you, your history, and your destiny.

O Jamaica your mother was an African queen; and your father a proud "masha."

And you have drunken yourself with their blood and stolen the hearts of my men.

You have openly seduced and recaptured my daughter's heart,

And now she, too, spills her blood for the life of your sons and daughters.

And now I can only say, "It's in her blood!"

And though my heart shudders with fear as my child moves fearlessly through your sin-scarred streets and searches for your sin-scarred children,

And though my heart leaps as my husband-man pays his just covenant dues and more, and burns with love for your cities and its children,

And though his gentle heart and spirit would rise in anger at the blatant oppression of his people

And the senseless, lawless recklessness which runs rampant in his nation's streets,

Still my greatest joy, and

Still my fervent mother's prayer is to see my children walk free

With heads held high with island pride and their children, too, walk free and say, "Your fathers were this nation's leaders, its brave defenders!"

And "This is my beloved, blessed fatherland, and You its Eternal Father!"

Appendix A
My Beloved Son:
A Prophet

How to Raise Your Sons as Prophets

A long, long time before a prophet's birth, a young girl's heart races into the future,

Her spirit fed by the history of her past and captured by the call of destiny,

Her hope fueled by the repeated promise of the Father God to bless her fathers' seed because of the promise that He had made to her fathers' fathers...

And generations before a prophet's seed of life is thrust into the world, a young man's dream becomes a vision.

No longer does he only relive the past with its prevailing darkness lit up only by the spark of covenant of the Creator God, whose promise to restore is always linked to the birth of a son.

But now this man envisions the future and sees his own son's life becoming one of those sparks, no, a flame of light for his own generation.

And so a son of hope and vision is birthed.

What child is this? Whose son are you?

For in the brilliant light of a searching Father God you were exposed; your heart fashioned after the likeness of the Son of God; your limbs made strong and numbered one by one, your soul encased in the same supple bands of compassion; and your spirit set apart, named, anointed; and yes, your very life infused with a driven, unsatisfied desire to see mercy, truth, and justice restored; and the hand of God's judgment removed; and the glory of the created match the glory of their Creator!

What child is this? Whose son are you?

Again the parents ask.

This son is different. So often misunderstood.

Is this preoccupation?

Why does he so often seem to drift into his own world?

Or is this some inner, persistent call to which he is summoned?

He seems to ponder the affairs of life so deeply and

He seems to intrude into the concerns of man so boldly and

His eyes and heart wander so often in the direction of the cry of the people...

How often is he misunderstood...Is his a prophet's spirit?

His nature...why so angry at times?

Why this fierce opposing of perceived injustice?

His meekness...Is it weakness?

Why does he not speak up for himself, defend himself as he defends the rest?

His withdrawal...Is it fear?

Why does he so often seek the quiet and, yes, the lonely place?

Is he not "Mary's" son? Why does he then walk around with head held high, with an air of greatness thrust upon him,

And with a sense of being that separates him from the rest?

His words…how sharp and incisive they are!

They cut into the very fiber of all the strongholds of men.

They expose the broken covenants and the shameful, lustful, prideful indifference of men.

And how clearly does this prophet's son speak of his Father's love,

In one breath he trumpets out his Father's judgment and laments the Father's broken heart.

And yes, in the same breath he pleads, as only the Father could, for men to return to the God of their fathers.

What child is this? Whose son are you?

And how tenderly must I wean you and whisper in your little ear:

"You are the Father's child.

How much you look like Him!

You are the Prophet's son.

How much you grow into His likeness.

I shall instill into your little heart the love of the Father

And obedience to the call of destiny.

I shall pour into your little spirit the love of the people.

I shall overwhelm you with the sense of the future,

And I shall remind you often of who you are."

And yes, I, too, shall be prepared to be judged by your incisive words.

I, too, shall store up and ponder in my own heart the words which seem to come from deep inside the agelessness of your spirit.

And as Hannah did, I shall yearly make an ephod for you.

I shall stand apart and watch you grow into what you were called to be—prophet of God.

You shall hear the call of God and quickly discern His voice;

And you shall answer, "Speak, Lord, for thy servant heareth."

You shall bless what your God has blessed,

And you shall stand aside and not weep for that which God has cursed.

You shall hear the cries of the people,

And with blind obedience you shall follow your God.

And yes…your father and I shall have hope restored.

For this our child, our son, has found his true Fatherhood.

His "Thus saith the Lord!" will sound forth unhindered, hill and free.

Appendix B
My Beloved Son: A Priest

How to Raise Your Sons as Priests

On behalf of the people,

The masses, without hope, without will and without law

On behalf of the people,

Offering sacrifices of atonement, of repentance, and of thanksgiving

On behalf of the people,

Renewing daily God's mercy, offering daily the Father's forgiveness,

You, my child, called to be the priest of the Most High God.

With what do I clothe you? How must I shape your head?

How must I fan the flame of the candle of the priesthood which burns within your spirit?

First, I will tell you of your history, of the past of our forefathers.

God's finger as surely on their lives as it is on yours this day.

I will tell you of one who in the ancient civilizations of his African past offered to his ancestral spirits the people's incense.

I will tell you of another who in the Amazon jungles of his South American past was priest unto his Indian people.

I will tell you of one who in the teaming ricelands of the China mainland offered sacrifices to the multi-named god of the many faces;

Of the ones who, with blind devotion and catholic symbolism, were separated to the priesthood because in their spirits shone that holy light which sometimes blinds me when I look at you!

And why all of this? Generations of priests!

Spawning sons of willing, priestly vessels sanctified and set apart for the Master's use.

As I watch your father priest, I well remember the priests of my own ancestry, and my heart trembles with holy anticipation and some fear.

The smell of holy incense warms my heart and makes my body willing to have a seed-priest implanted there for I, too, need your sacrifices unto God and on behalf of my people.

For as surely as the God of your fathers blessed and separated them for service, so are you called by Him, my son.

At your birth I saw within your eyes a tiny flame of God's candlestick, and I knew that this one was born to be a priest of God.

One single generational call that ties you to the heart of God and dominates your entire life. One generational claim upon the seed of my fathers and upon my own seed!

No inheritance as others crave for it

For God is your inheritance. No striving for honor as others strive,

For worthy of double honor are you.

No scathing curses for the people who sin, and sacrifice, and return to sin, and return to sacrifice.

For you see their repentance, and you see as well the mercy of the God in whose place you stand.

When others condemn, you offer the Father's forgiveness.

When others pass by on the other side, you stop to pour on the oil of healing.

When others cannot bear the weight of the sin of this dying people, you lift that burden and offer that sacrifice and drench your own self in the atoning blood of Jesus.

And so my task is made easy, for your call is loud and clear.

Unhindered by greed or care, you will wash yourself clean and submit yourself to a life of priestly preparation.

But as for me, I will daily fan the little flame which at your birth I saw.

I will teach you to love the people and to feel their pain.

I will train you to discern the heart of your God, who waits for pure and reasonable sacrifices.

I will help you to fear the wrath of our God, who hates the sins of the people and who turns at the cry of the oppressed.

I will warn you to follow exactly, closely, and without wavering the prescribed law of the Holy God.

I will watch you closely as you curb your own flesh, and discipline your own body, and bend your own supple spirit…

For you must live in the world of men, women, and sin and have lust for nothing except to see men set free, to see God's glory exposed, and to hear God's voice.

And when you enter the Most Holy Place and talk with your God face-to-face,

Then I shall wait to hear those little bells I patiently sewed into the hem of your priestly garment

And you, my son, will step backward from the presence of your God.

And again into the world of your people and on their behalf be what you were born to be—a priest of the Most High!

Appendix C
My Beloved Son:
A King

How to Raise Your Sons as Kings

Earmarked for kingship, the stamp of royalty on their hearts.

Their brows open and clear, carrying the mark of the Most High King, the Sovereign Lord.

Their hearts made strong, their spirits brave

And their souls eager for the taste of victory.

No fear lurks in the shadows of their souls

No tarnished vision of the goals ahead

No greed to conquer lands they must not rule

No sideward glances at the trivial pursuits.

And how easily we can identify these young dominion kings!

This one—with that aloof and somewhat distant spirit!

How piercing are his eyes! How closely he scans the affairs of men and screens out all the dross and masquerades!

He steps back from idle debate and purposeless chatter

And searches until he finds that single morsel of truth from out of all the cacophony of men's talk.

And understanding dawns

And this young king absorbs only the deeper understanding of truths

That can find in his treasure heart of knowledge a link with his reservoir of wisdom!

His meat is to do the will of the Father and to obey,

That persistent ever-prodding call of destiny to execute change in his world, to right the wrongs of all his fathers,

And to sound a strident judgment call to tolerated oppressors and oppression.

This young king—I can see him from a distance

So calm but ever searching eyes…a mild haughtiness that laughs a little laugh

Which then turns itself into an inner abiding locking of the spirit,

Into a deep reserve of self-sustained confidence.

An all-entrancing distancing of the world.

He bounces into view with full stride—man of the world, yet one framed from beyond

From beyond the reach of ordinary creatures—my child of destiny!

How well you are to learn the lessons of the wise!

Do not give your heart away to strange loves.

Do not meddle in the business of petty men.

Do not judge according to the devices of your heart.

Withhold not your hand of judgment from the rich

And turn not away your hand of mercy from the poor.

Weep with the widow and laugh with the bride,

For they speak to you of the sorrows and joys of your people.

Go not the way of the seducing one, whose motive is to weaken the knees of kings; to entrap them in the web of sweet perfumes and mocking lies; and whose end is that of senseless, wanton, careless death.

And yes! Young kings, learn well the sounds of victory.

And hunger for that for which you were born and that for which you move and have your being:

—the happy, free laughter of your nation's children

—the strong, victorious shouts of your nation's men

—the fearless, rejoicing songs of your nation's women

And the battle cries of victory and the exulting sounds of praise to the King of all Kings to whom you, too, must bow!

Appendix D
The Morgan Wisdom Scale

by Dr. C. Patricia Morgan, Ph. D.
Educational Psychologist
Specialist in Education

Please complete items 1 through 5.

1. Name______________________ 2. Date ________________

3. Date of birth _______________________

4. Name of person scoring this scale ______________________

5. Relationship to child (circle one)

(a) Mother (b) Father (c) Teacher (d) Other _________

First, read this definition of wisdom.

WISDOM

Wisdom is knowing and loving God, obeying God and His Word, acting by what you know God's Word says, and wanting only to please God, your Father. The wise child has many blessings in store for him or her. To be wise means to hear, learn, understand, remember, and obey God's instructions. You act wisely when you remember consequences and make right decisions based on that knowledge. Wisdom is easy when you love God and those persons whom God has placed over you as Christian parents and teachers. Wisdom is remembering time-tested principles, morals, and values and acting with a sense of purpose and destiny.

Now, read the following directions.

For each item first read the Scripture or Wisdom Key. Then read the statement. Then score yourself out of five. The score should reflect the extent to which the statement is true for you. The higher the score, the more the statement is true. Be truthful. Do not leave out any. Total the scores for the 25 items. Next, identify your present level of functioning and your growth in wisdom. Turn to the last page of this form and use the formula to compute the Wisdom Quotient (WQ).

For further instruction, see pages 174–176.

Now turn the page and begin.

	Statement	Rating Out of 5	Key Scripture References
1.	Learning is enjoyable to me.		*"When wisdom entereth into thine heart, and knowledge is pleasant unto thy soul."* (Prov. 2:10)
2.	I make decisions based on well-learned biblical principles.		*"Discretion shall preserve thee, understanding shall keep thee: to deliver thee."* (Prov. 2:11–12)
3.	I am reaping the reward of my study and learning.		*"And by knowledge shall the chambers be filled with all precious and pleasant riches."* (Prov. 24:4)
4.	I am being trained to value knowledge and understanding.		*"Train up a child in the way he should go: and when he is old, he will not depart from it."* (Prov. 22:6)
5.	I can describe my life as being "built" and "established."		*"Every wise* [man] *buildeth* [his] *house."* (Prov. 14:1) *"Through wisdom is an house builded; and by understanding it is established."* (Prov. 24:3)
6.	I obey my parents' advice about pursuing study or learning.		*"My son, if thou wilt receive my words...so that thou incline thine ear unto wisdom...Then shalt thou understand."* (Prov. 2:1–2, 5)
7.	I have the fear of the Lord.		*"The fear of the LORD is the beginning of knowledge: but fools despise wisdom and instruction."* (Prov. 1:7) *"The fear of the LORD is the beginning of wisdom: and the knowledge of the holy is understanding."* (Prov. 9:10)

Statement	Rating Out of 5	Key Scripture References
8. My best friends and companions pursue knowledge and understanding.		*"He that walketh with wise men shall be wise: but a companion of fools shall be destroyed."* (Prov. 13:20)
9. I am not lazy, and I do not put off doing things.		*"The soul of the sluggard desireth, and hath nothing: but the soul of the diligent shall be made fat."* (Prov. 13:4) (Also see Proverbs 6:6–11.)
10. I never talk a lot.		*"But he that refraineth his lips is wise."* (Prov. 10:19). *"There is that speaketh like the piercings of a sword: but the tongue of the wise is health."* (Prov. 12:18) *"Wise men lay up knowledge: but the mouth of the foolish is near destruction."* (Prov. 10:14)
11. I never tell lies.		*"Have not I* [wisdom] *written to thee excellent things in counsels and knowledge, that I might make thee know the certainty of the words of truth; that thou mightest answer the words of truth to them that send unto thee?"* (Prov. 22:20–21)
12. I continually try to increase my learning and my skills.		*"A wise man will hear, and will increase learning."* (Prov. 1:5)
13. I am not easily enticed.		*"For the LORD giveth wisdom"* (Prov. 2:6) *"That thou mayest walk in the way of good men, and keep the paths of the righteous."* (Prov. 2:20)

Statement	Rating Out of 5	Key Scripture References
14. I do not have fear of evil.		*"But whoso hearkeneth unto me* [wisdom] *shall dwell safely, and shall be quiet from fear of evil."* (Prov. 1:33)
15. I have good favor and success in the sight of God and man.		*"So shalt thou find favour and good understanding in the sight of God and man."* (Prov. 3:4)
16. I am healthy.		*"It shall be health to thy navel* [body], *and marrow to thy bones."* (Prov. 3:8)
17. I enjoy getting more knowledge and know that I will prosper.		*"My son, eat thou honey, because it is good; and the honeycomb, which is sweet to thy taste: so shall the knowledge of wisdom be unto thy soul: when thou hast found it, then there shall be a reward, and thy expectation shall not be cut off."* (Prov. 24:13–14)
18. I listen to the instruction of my father, and I do not forsake the law of my mother.		*"My son, hear the instruction of thy father, and forsake not the law of thy mother."* (Prov. 1:8)
19. I honor the Lord by my giving.		*"Honour the* Lord *with thy substance, and with the firstfruits of all thine increase: so shall thy barns be filled with plenty, and thy presses shall burst out with new wine."* (Prov. 3:9–10)
20. I always listen to good advice.		*"Cease, my son, to hear the instruction that causeth to err from the words of knowledge"* (Prov. 19:27)

Statement	Rating Out of 5	Key Scripture References
21. I am doing those things that will give me a rich inheritance.		*"I lead in the way of righteousness, in the midst of the paths of judgment: that I may cause those that love me to inherit substance; and I will fill their treasures."* (Prov. 8:20–21)
22. I always walk in the way of life.		*"There is a way which seemeth right unto a man, but the end thereof are the ways of death."* (Prov. 14:12)
23. My parents or guardians rejoice over me because of my wise actions and words.		*"The father of the righteous shall greatly rejoice: and he that begetteth a wise child shall have joy of him."* (Prov. 23:24)
24. I can control myself.		*"He that hath no rule over his own spirit is like a city that is broken down, and without walls."* (Prov. 25:28)
25. I use my gifts and talents.		*"A man's gift maketh room for him, and bringeth him before great men."* (Prov. 18:16)

Compute Your Wisdom Quotient (WQ)

Use this formula: $WQ = \frac{\text{The obtained score}}{125} \times \frac{100}{1}$

(Maximum Potential Score)

Then rate yourself using the classification table.

WQ	Classification	Level of Wisdom
90-100	Superior; gifted	Wise
80-89	High average	Good growth in wisdom
70-79	Average	Uneven or slow growth
60-69	Low average	Borderline deficient
59 and below	Below average	Deficient

Obtained Score____________
WQ____________
Classification________________

Now, read this:

This score reflects your present functioning. It is an indication of areas of strength and of weakness. Now check again to see where growth is slow. Work on these areas and improve your wisdom level. Each item represents a particular domain or area that may need some more work. As you do this, you will maximize your spiritual development and your educational potential. After six or seven months, you may wish to measure your wisdom growth again!

Appendix E
The Individualized Purpose Plan

by Dr. C. Patricia Morgan, Ph. D.
Educational Psychologist
Specialist in Education

Your child is a Child of Destiny.
The purpose for each child is an eternal one, determined before the foundation of the world. When this purpose is identified, all caregivers are to pursue determined goals for the greatest fulfillment of maximized potential.

When purpose is not identified and potential maximized, abuse and failure are inevitable.

The IPP is subdivided in twelve major sections.

I. INTRODUCTION AND GUIDELINES FOR USE
II. BIOGRAPHICAL DATA
III. FAMILY AND GENETIC INHERITANCE
IV. FAMILY TREE
V. FAMILY TALENTS AND GIFTS
VI. NATURAL GIFTS, ABILITIES, AND POTENTIAL
VII. DECLARATIONS AND BLESSINGS
VIII. PARENTS' BLESSINGS OR PROPHETIC DECLARATIONS
IX. DIRECTIONAL WORDS RECEIVED FROM OTHERS
X. PLANNING FOR ACHIEVEMENT OF THE CHILD'S PURPOSE
XI. GENERAL PURPOSE PLANNING FORM
XII. INDIVIDUALIZED PURPOSE PLAN FORM

I. INSTRUCTION AND GUIDELINES

The Individualized Purpose Plan (IPP) organizes and accurately identifies and defines a child's purpose and life goals; it programs for the maximizing of that child's potential.

This plan, the IPP, has a similar format to the time-tested Individualized Education Plan (IEP) currently used with great success by parents and educators of children with special needs.

The IPP is a planning and record-keeping instrument. It should become part of a child's/student's culmulative file. The following are simple guidelines for its use:

1. The IPP is to be completed by parents for each child.
2. Other significant caregivers and teachers are to participate in the formation of the IPP.
3. The IPP is to be used as a foundational instrument to plan programs for education, life skills, training, and all social, familial, and spiritual/moral development.
4. Information is to be collected by careful research and by thoughtful consideration of all pertinent information concerning the child.
5. Once the data has been gathered by this careful process, the material will become an important document or tool upon which this child's future life goals will be planned. Success depends upon the dynamic and ongoing use of this document as a working tool.
6. New directions or fuller understanding or knowledge of the child's purpose will be added to the IPP. New program changes will be designed or redesigned to ensure accurate execution of all plans.
7. Provision of all resources must be ensured. These may include, for example:

a. New school change for educational enhancement of a special child.

b. Residential adjustment/change to secure appropriate accomodation of the vision and purpose plan for the child.

c. Provision of training for the talented or gifted child—for example, tutoring services for a young musician/artist.

d. Arrangements for visits to watch parliamentary proceedings (if one child's life goal is to become a lawyer or statesman).

8. This IPP also provides the necessary planning forms for clearly stated long- and short-term goals. They are simple forms and are easily completed.
9. The extent to which stated goals have been attained is also tracked. A parent, teacher, or significant caregiver is required to determine the success score (out of 100%). This will determine the next move—to move ahead with the plan or to repeat the process in order to ensure IPP effectiveness.
10. Parents are to meet with other significant persons, including teachers, every three or four months for an IPP conference. The goals will be:

a. to assess goal alignment to major objectives.

b. to determine the extent to which short-term goals/objectives have been completed.

c. to collaborate on plans for the future.

d. to ensure that all caregivers are actively involved in the purposeful development of the child.

II. BIOGRAPHICAL DATA

Date today: ____________

Child's Name: ________________________

Meaning of child's names (if known):

____

____

Name of father: ______________________

Name of mother: ______________________

Name of current caregiver: _______________

Relationship to child: __________

Number of children in family: ____

Place of child in family: _____

Child's date of birth: __________Grade in school:______

Child's age: ______ Name of school:__________________

How would you describe this child? (circle one)

Gifted / Superior / Above Average / Average / Below Average / Well Below Average

Signature of persons completing this IPP

Parent __________________ Parent _________________

Teacher __________________ Teacher _________________

III. FAMILY AND GENETIC INHERITANCE

Inherited Potential and Strengths

A child's potential, gift, or talent is often inherited. Your child may have a genetic predisposition or innate ability that is also possessed by a parent or other relative. The gift may have been observed in a grandparent, a great grandparent, or another family member.

IV. FAMILY TREE

Complete this Family Tree with names.

Child's Name: ________________

Date: ________________

Father	**Mother**
Name: ________________	Name: ________________
Paternal	**Maternal**
Grandfather's Name: ________________	Grandfather's Name: ________________
Grandmother's Name: ________________	Grandmother's Name: ________________
Grandfather's Father's Name: ________________	Grandfather's Father's Name: ________________
Grandfather's Mother's Name: ________________	Grandfather's Mother's Name: ________________
Grandmother's Father's Name: ________________	Grandmother's Father's Name: ________________
Grandmother's Mother's Name: ________________	Grandmother's Mother's Name: ________________

V. FAMILY TALENTS AND GIFTS

Now think of any strengths, special gifts, or talents of persons in your family tree. Write them below and put a check mark where you see that ability or potential in this child.

Mother	Father
______________________	______________________
Maternal Grandmother	Paternal Grandmother
______________________	______________________
Maternal Grandfather	Paternal Grandfather
______________________	______________________
Maternal Great Grandmother	Paternal Great Grandmother
______________________	______________________
Maternal Great Grandfather	Paternal Great Grandfather
______________________	______________________
Other Close Relative	Other Close Relative
______________________	______________________
Other Close Relative	Other Close Relative
______________________	______________________

VI. NATURAL GIFTS, ABILITIES, AND POTENTIAL

Every significant caregiver is able to notice a child's gifting, natural abilities, or special talents. These are basic, powerful indicators of a child's leadership qualities and his/her potential. Identifying these natural abilities also helps us determine what tools of training the child would need to develop the life skills necessary for the fulfillment of his/her purpose.

Parents are encouraged to observe their child and to identify abilities and potential. They are now asked to *name* and *affirm* these gifts and abilities by clearly defining them.

Complete the following and put a check mark in the small column in the center where a plan has to be put in place. For each ability or gift checked, complete the section on the right called Plans for Development. Write out what is to be done to ensure that goals will be achieved and that the child's purpose will be fulfilled.

This Child's Natural Abilities, Special Gifts, or Potential	√	Plans for Development
1.		1.
2.		2.
3.		3.
4.		4.
5.		5.
6.		6.
7.		7.

VII. DECLARATIONS AND BLESSINGS

This section deals with the powerful gift each parent has—to bless or declare good success in the future life of a child.

1. One gift a parent may give a child is that of a blessing.
2. To bless a child means to give a good gift to that child.
3. To bless also means to speak words concerning the future of that child. The words come with the parent's goodwill and desire to see that child prosper in all areas and be in good health.
4. A parent's blessing places and calls forth specific rulership ability in children.
5. A parent's blessing activates success, prosperity, and creativity in children.
6. A parent's blessing overrules every negative declaration spoken over a child.
7. The love behind a blessing becomes a driving force or a strong impetus, which causes the good word of blessing to become fulfilled.
8. Any parent or adult who speaks a blessing or who makes declarations concerning future events will also endeavor to provide resources and opportunities for that child to inherit those blessings.
9. These blessings and words spoken should be recorded and remembered. They should be used to continually maximize support and enhance motivation for that child to become all that he or she was born to become.

VIII. PARENTS' BLESSING OR PROPHETIC DECLARATIONS

A parent or the child's main caregiver has been entrusted with the awesome task of nurturing that child toward the fulfillment of his/her purpose. It is important for that person to listen to his/her inner voice and to receive direction and guidance. Next, all such prophetic directions are meditated on, and the parent, with wisdom, determines exactly what he/she believes is a clear word and what the important directional promises for that child are.

The following is a statement of the promises for a child that the parents have already received. These directional and specific words act as guidelines for determining the future of that child. They were revealed directly to the parents/caregivers and are to be stated and given definition.

The following helps the one completing this form to recall the directional promises and to relate them to the specific, ordained purpose for that child. These prophetic words or blessings may have been given before or after a child's birth or at special occassion events such as infant dedication, christening, or a birthday celebration.

	Year/Date the Prophetic Word Was Received	On the Occasion of	A Summary of the Guiding Words Concerning this Child's Purpose or Future
1.			
2.			
3.			
4.			
5.			
6.			

IX. DIRECTIONAL WORDS RECEIVED FROM OTHERS

Prophetic and directional words are also revealed to other significant persons apart from the child's main caregiver. The persons may be relatives, a child's spiritual leader or pastor, or family friends. The prophecies may have been given on the occasion of a baby dedication, a birthday, or in a family or church meeting.

It is important for the parents to record the promises which they believe are significant. These are the prophecies that will usually bring hope, inner conviction, and confirmation of other words already given for that child. Parents are urged to listen to test every word and to trust their inner source of truth to guide their actions. Next, they are to carefully record these prophetic words.

The following is a record of the main words of blessing or direction given or spoken by others. The persons completing this IPP are to carefully recall these.

	Year/Date the Promise/Word was Received/Spoken by a Person Other Than the Parent	On the Occasion of	A Summary of the Prophetic Word Concering this Child's Purposes
1.			
2.			
3.			
4.			
5.			
6.			

X. PLANNING FOR ACHIEVEMENT OF THE CHILD'S PURPOSE

It is now easy to identify major long-term goals for your child's fulfillment of life goals and purpose.

A. Look back at the forms already completed. These include the Family and Hereditary Potential, A Child's Natural Gifts and Abilities, and Special Words of Blessing Given for the Child by Parents or by Others.

B. Decide on areas of Identified Purpose and Potential. For example, my child is called to be "a musician," "an artist," "a wise counselor." My child has "a strong verbal ability," and is called to develop as "a national leader," "an outstanding athlete," or "a good accountant." Call these "major goals."

C. To fully train a child to achieve great success demands that all areas are given attention. Plans will have to be put in place for spiritual development, educational development, special gifts and talent training, social/ emotional development, and physical development.

Complete the following form where you name major goals, career goals, or the purpose and call on your child's life. You may wish to prioritize them.

XI. GENERAL PURPOSE PLANNING FORM

Major Goals

To become a

1. ______________________________
2. ______________________________
3. ______________________________

To be a leader in the area of

1. ______________________________
2. ______________________________
3. ______________________________

To achieve success in

1. ______________________________
2. ______________________________
3. ______________________________

The parents, teacher, and any other significant caregiver can together develop the IPP. The major Areas for Development are listed on the next page. This grid will form your basic and overall Individualized Purpose Plan.

Use the information already collected to develop the following instrument.

MAJOR GOALS	AREAS FOR DEVELOPMENT				
	Spiritual and Moral Development	Educational Development	Special Gifts and Talents Education and Training	Social/Emotional Development	Physical Development

XII. INDIVIDUALIZED PURPOSE PLANNING FORM

The next step is to complete the actual program planning form. Look back at the previous page and identify which of the areas you want to begin with. Enter or write down these areas of development and identified Major Goals. Next, list your short-term goals or clear steps to get to your goal.

INDIVIDUALIZED PURPOSE PLAN
PROGRAM PLANNING FORM

Area of Development: ____________________ Date: ____________

Major Goal: ____

Signature of Person Completing this Form: ____

SHORT-TERM GOALS	RESOURCES NEEDED Activities to Be Planned	% ACHIEVED	FOLLOW-UP PLANS
1. ____________________ ____________________ ____________________			
2. ____________________ ____________________ ____________________			
3. ____________________ ____________________ ____________________			